I Remember—

Stories by United Methodist

Deaconesses and Missionaries

CALLED SERVED

SERVING STILL

Compiled and edited by

Esther L. Megill

Cover Design

Sylvia Cottingham Smyth

authorHOUSE®

AuthorHouse™
1663 Liberty Drive
Bloomington, IN 47403
www.authorhouse.com
Phone: 1 (800) 839-8640

Published by AuthorHouse 09/29/2016

ISBN: 978-1-5246-4048-4 (sc)
ISBN: 978-1-5246-4047-7 (e)

Library of Congress Control Number: 2016915588

Print information available on the last page.

Preface

Brooks-Howell Home, established in 1957, is a retirement community for deaconesses and missionaries of The United Methodist Church. Brooks-Howell Home is owned and governed by United Methodist Women. Admission is open to retirees and staff of the United Methodist Women (formerly Women's Division), missionaries of the former National and World Divisions (now the General Board of Global Ministries) and others approved for residency. A majority of the residents are missionaries and deaconesses.

For many years a bi-monthly newsletter, the *Serendipitor*, has been published. Among the articles there are a number called "I Remember." These are stories of memorable events during their time of active service, written by deaconesses and missionaries. It is these (plus a few older ones written before "I Remember" began) which have been compiled and prepared for publication in this book. We trust that you will find them interesting—some humorous, perhaps some sad, but all of interest to you.

Brooks-Howell Home, front entrance

Table of Contents

I Remember. 48

Memories of Christmas

So Many Christmases

In the picturesque hill country of Fukien Province, the Methodists had a mission station at Kutien. There, each year, we celebrated not one, but several Christmases.

I can still see Martha Graf standing on a chair, festooning decorations over the doors and windows of our home. A tiny tree intertwined with lights and decked out with diminutive birds and angels graced the living room center table.

The first Christmas, early, we invited over the women from the weaving school. They sat around the table in a polite, stiff group, until Martha darkened the room and switched on the tree lights. With gasps of delight the women relaxed enough to enjoy the carols, games, tea and cookies, and join in the closing prayer.

The second Christmas came on the eve when the girls of our two high schools put on their banquet and program. Then they scattered to circle the compound all night long in joyous comradeship, singing carols and calling greetings under every window.

The third Christmas, on The Day, our primary school pupils rose before dawn to parade through the streets carrying lighted paper lanterns and singing carols at the homes of church members. Their feast was served at noon.

During the year senior students fanned out to nearby villages holding Bible classes for children each Sunday. On one day, with mounting excitement, they gathered their little charges into the school playing ground for the fourth Christmas. Against a backdrop of feathery bamboo, the youngsters recited Bible verses, sang hymns and carols, and said the prayers they had learned. Then came games, small gifts and refreshments. After taking the children home, our weary girls, glowing with satisfaction, returned to the compound. For them, this last Christmas was the best, for it was the Christmas they had given away.

Marion Holmes
Missionary to China, Malaysia, Sarawak
(Methodist Episcopal Church)
1931-1950, 1957-1964
(Submitted 1981)

Cuba

In Matanzas, Cuba, years ago, the boarding pupils had gone home for Christmas holidays. Another teacher, some of the kitchen staff and I were left in our school. A few days before Christmas the cook said to me, "Come see what we have in the yard."

Outside, I saw two fine, big turkeys. "Where did these come from?" I wanted to know.

"From the Perez family. They raised the turkeys in their back yard," the cook replied.

I knew the Perez family was very poor. They had a little girl in our school on full scholarship. I was almost in tears. I foolishly asked, "Couldn't we send the turkeys back, so that the family could sell them or have one for Christmas dinner?"

The cook shook her head, "No," she said, "we couldn't because they are a gift of gratitude."

I believe I shall never forget that sacrificial "gift of gratitude."

Juanita Kelly
Missionary to Cuba, Argentina
1932-1960, 1961-1963
(Methodist Episcopal Church, The Methodist Church)
(Submitted 1987)

Zaire (Congo)

It was Christmas Eve in the Congo, Africa. We sat under a star-lit sky to enjoy a presentation, in drama and music, of the birth of Christ. The shepherds' field was on a deserted ant-hill. The sheep were there (but had no wool). Bethlehem's stables with Joseph, Mary and her baby, were seen in the distance. Angels proclaimed the glad news. A tin-foil star led the travelers to the manger. Three Wisemen, dressed in colorful robes, sang "We Three Kings." They presented their gifts.

Christmas morning we gathered in the chapel to worship and present our gifts to the Christ, such things as baskets of rice, tropical fruit, chickens and eggs were placed on the altar. Some brought Congo franks.

One lady waited and then came and said, "I have nothing to bring to my Lord except myself." She then knelt and gave herself, her all, to Christ.

Annimae White
1930-1965
Missionary to Zaire
(Methodist Episcopal Church, South; The Methodist Church)
(Submitted 1987)

Brazil

The students called it the "open Jungle," since they felt they had come from the "closed jungle." All were Christian and had come to learn how to live and work in their own churches. To them, Christmas was celebrated with prayer and worship until midnight, December 24. Everyone was working diligently to prepare the gifts.

On Christmas Day we took our gifts to a family who had never heard of Jesus. We explained—some people had a party and gave gifts to recognize their children's birthdays. Today is Jesus' birthday, so we give gifts to others. We have brought this dress and shirt material for you in celebration of Jesus' birthday. After each of us had explained in various ways the meaning of Christmas, we left. As we were closing the yard gate, two of the children came running, saying, "You forgot your package!"

Well, it took many weeks to cultivate and win the confidence and friendship of this family – to develop their awareness of the concept of Christmas giving, and who Jesus is. But a start had been made!

Gladys Oberlin
Missionary Brazil 1943-1976
Volunteer in Brazil 1977-1981
(The Methodist Church, United Methodist Church)
(Submitted 1987)

4

Philippines and Samoa

Christmas is celebrated similarly in these two areas—church service, caroling in the neighborhood, midnight feast.

At Aldersgate, the first tri-lingual church in Hawaii, these customs were reenacted one year when I was present. The people met together in their traditional neighborhood program; carols were sung in four languages—Ilocono, Samoan, Portuguese and English. A grass shack was constructed to hold the manger scene, with a Filipino star hung over it.

Singing was followed by the Christmas story dramatization: Mary was a neighborhood Hawaiian girl; Joseph and the shepherds were Samoan and Portuguese; the wisemen, Filipinos; and the baby was the five-day old son of a local Samoan congregation pastor. The baby slept through the drama, lying in a palm frond basket made by a Samoan woman. Children and adults were surprised to find a live baby when they brought their white gifts to his basket.

Truly this was an unforgettable Christmas experience for me.

Martha Almon
Deaconess-U.S.A.
1938- 1945, 1948-1976
(Methodist Episcopal Church, South;
The Methodist Church, United Methodist Church)

(Submitted 1987)

Nigeria

It is now dark—early evening—on Christmas Eve in the two villages of Filiya and Gbwandum just at the foot of the Pero hills in northeastern Nigeria. The women are home with the little children, but the men are beginning to gather at the church—each carrying a lantern for light.

A short worship service, in honor of the One whose birth they will be singing and telling about this night, is held. Then the events of the night begin. The men form small groups—some going to village compounds on the plain, the others to compounds of those living on the hills. At each place the story of the Christ Child, who came for all people—including them—is told and carols are sung. Then on to another place. This continues <u>all night</u> until dawn of Christmas day.

As I would awaken during the night I could always hear singing coming from somewhere—songs telling of the birth of Jesus.

Lucy Rowe
Missionary Nigeria 1946-1952, 1957-1963;
Sarawak, Malaysia 1964-1968
(Evangelical Church, Evangelical United Brethren Church,
United Methodist Church)

(Submitted1987)

Puerto Rico –where two Christmases are celebrated

 On December 25 the children have their gifts, Santa Claus and a Christmas tree much like in the USA. January 6 is the traditional "Three Kings Day" for everyone. On January 5 the children collect grass and put it in a box under their bed. If they have been good, when the Three Kings come that night the camels eat the grass and leave a present in the box. If the children have been bad, the grass is still in the box in the morning.

Early in December loud speakers can be heard in the Plaza playing Christmas carols. Nativity scenes are put up in homes and churches, but the Baby Jesus is not put in the crèche until Christmas Day. After January 6 everything except the Baby Jesus is removed from the crèche. The Baby stays for 40 days—representing the time Jesus was taken to Simeon and Anna in the temple.

Doris Armes
Deaconess—USA 1944-1984
The Methodist Church, United Methodist Church)
(Submitted 1987)

Hong Kong

"Joy to the World, the Lord is come." Shops, schools churches and homes (poor and rich alike—hillside squatters, houseboat homes, Methodist Villages (Wesley, Asbury and Epworth), rooftop schools—all gaily decorated in red and green during Advent, and many will remain so until Chinese New Year late in January or early February. Poinsettias, being inexpensive, are used extravagantly. Our school children got acquainted with Matthew's and Luke's first Christmas stories and several Christmas carols.

Women's literacy classes memorize John 3:16, "God so loved the world that He gave His own son that whoever believes in Him shall not perish but have eternal life." They love to share this verse in programs.

Some Chinese churches celebrate Jesus' birthday as they do their own by having a meal of steaming bowls of noodle soup flavored with either pork, chicken or beef. Ooh! So good! This meal is followed by a lovely worship service. Then Big Santa and Little Santa (dressed exactly alike) distribute gifts to everyone. No wonder they sing "Joy to the World."

Louise Avett
Missionary China 1932-1936, 1938-1945
Hong Kong 1960-1970
(Methodist Episcopal Church, The Methodist Church
United Methodist Church)
(Submitted 1987)

Japan

The percentage of Christians in Japan is 3% or less, leading someone to remark, on seeing displays in the department stores, that Japan may not be Christianized but it is certainly becoming "Christmas-ized." As I would go along the Ginza-Tokyo's shopping street, I would hear "Silent Night and "I'm Dreaming of a White Christmas" from loud speakers on telephone poles along the street. When I entered one of the large department stores, I was welcomed with a large sign –"Merry Christmas"—in English. After buying a gift I would be asked, "Do you want the gift wrapped for Christmas or for the New Year?" If for Christmas, it was wrapped with white paper, and tied with a red ribbon. If for New Year, it was also wrapped in white paper with the symbol of a fish on it and tied with red string.

In Christian schools and churches the programs were very similar to the Christmas programs we have here. In the schools Christmas carols were sung and young people sometimes went out in groups and sang carols in their neighborhood. I remember especially at Seibi Gakuen school in Yokohama the singing of the "Hallelujah Chorus" in English. It is very difficult for Japanese to distinguish between the l and r sounds, so you can imagine it was not easy for the seventh graders, who had only begun their study of English, to learn not only the word "Hallelujah," but also "The Lord God Omnipotent Reigneth," and to sing it with the older students.

Helen Barns
Missionary Japan 1921-1967
(Methodist Protestant Church, The Methodist Church)

(Submitted 1987)

Mexico

For nine nights (representing the time it is thought it took Mary and Joseph to make the journey from Nazareth to Bethlehem), the adults had the POSADA--they went around the neighborhood singing and looking for the Christ Child. They would carry a tray on which was a crèche.

The children always enjoyed the PIÑATA—stone jars, in the shape of animals and filled with candy, which are then cracked, and the candy goes everywhere.

No matter how poor a family might be, they can always put on a good "show" at Christmas or any other religious festival. They do things on a large scale.

An illegitimate child of a mother who had died was brought to the mission school. She accepted me as her mother—a relationship which still holds today. She is now grown and has raised a family of Christian children, all good church workers.

We always had study hall until nine o'clock. On Friday evenings I would take the children to my room for Bible class. The children would read and then tell the meaning they gained from what they read. Christian services were held on Christmas as well as at other times.

Ola Callahan
Missionary Mexico 1928-1958
(Methodist Episcopal Church South; The Methodist Church)

(Submitted 1987)

India

I was always in charge of a boarding school. Most of the children went home for the Christmas holidays, but usually 20 or more stayed with me—some orphans and some children assigned to us by the Juvenile Court.

At Christmas I always gave them clothing plus a cloth bag containing a variety of needed items—with something they really wanted. One year when I asked them what they especially wanted, the little girls said they wanted some of the animals they could blow up and make stand on their feet. I had never seen such, so told them I did not know where to find them. They told me in the Bombay bazaar. So the next time I went to Bombay I looked and, sure enough, I found them—dog, horse, cow, lion, tiger. All were a nice size when blown up.

The older girls said they wanted a *Ghat* or *Nilgiri*. Again, I didn't know what they meant, but later learned these were the names of two kinds of face powder. So all the children had a most wonderful Christmas!

Leola Greene
Missionary India 1920-1955
(Methodist Episcopal Church; The Methodist Church)
(Submitted 1987)

Korea

During my first five years in Korea, 1925-1930, I lived in Songdo. It was a pleasant surprise to have Christmas carols sung to me during the night of December 24. At that time some Koreans sang to the missionaries.

In 1930-40 I lived in Chulwon. It was a smaller city and had only one church. Our single women missionaries usually invited other missionaries to spend the holidays with us. The thing that always surprised them was that on December 25 we had church services as on Sunday.

Eulene Weems
Missionary Korea 1925-1940; 1953-1965
(Methodist Episcopal Church, South; The Methodist Church)

(Submitted 1987)

Navajo Indian

Navajo Methodist Mission School's Christmas excitement was gone when the children went home to their families.

Then the pastor and wife invited the teachers to accompany them, the nurse and the student interpreter, to Burnham's Trading Post. There we could distribute Christmas goodies to the Navajos who came from miles around. Four teachers gratefully accepted. The station wagon and truck were filled with gifts--fruit, clothing, sweets--and people. The one-hour drive was shortened by conversation about the Indians we would meet, the program of gospel message and Navajo language hymns we would sing, and the scenery.

The mile-high country was cold! Warm clothing felt good as we walked among the people, smiling and greeting them. They wore long print skirts and jeans and brightly colored velveteen blouses decorated with silver and turquoise. Their Indian blankets kept them and their children warm.

The interpreter led all in singing; they listened to the reading from "God Bizaad" and the sermon. The true meaning of Christmas was presented, after which gifts were distributed.

We returned home feeling "a different way"—ready for our own Christmas.

Helen C. Wolfarth
Deaconess United States 1947-1953; 1972-1974
(The Methodist Church; United Methodist Church)

(Submitted 1987)

Memories of Early Years

Sharing at Depth

In the Pakur district in India where I worked some twenty years ago, we had a real village center in charge of an English nurse, Miss Sketchley. It was called Theodori Mission. It had a grade school, a church, and a dispensary. A few years ago the nurse opened a separate clinic for treatment of leprosy patients. She soon had 250 patients coming for treatment. I learned from her that in the district there were 25,000 known lepers.

When I was in India in 1926 the treatment for such patients was to give them injections of chalgugra oil. However, some years back a wonderful discovery of a new drug was made, which could be given by mouth—sulphone. It was found that through the use of sulphone leprosy patients who patiently and consistently took it—even those who had this illness for many years— can become free of this terrible disease.

I wish to quote a small portion of Miss Sketchley's report to the Conference: "It is impossible to find words to describe how it feels to be able to say to a leper 'You are clean.' There are no words to tell the emotion I felt the first time I had the privilege of handing a 'clean certificate' to one of our patients. This man had eaten his medicine for ten years—ten long, weary years. I only know that he received the reward of his perseverance and patience. The expression of joy on his face is something I will remember as long as I live. . . but there is a tragic side of this work also, like the old man who had been declared clean but who had only started to take treatment after his hands and feet were deformed and crippled. He took his clean certificate from my hand and said with much bitterness in his voice, 'How can you say I am clean? Look at my hands! Look at my feet! No one will ever believe that I am clean even if I do have a certificate to prove that I am.'"

A few years ago the Government began to take over work among lepers. Some Mission centers did hand over their patients to the government doctor. In Theodori, Miss Sketchley found her patients did not want to go to the government doctors. She asked them why and said that the medicine was the same. They replied, "The medicine can be the same, but the hands are different." She learned that the man dispensing the medicine for the government would go around in a Jeep. He remained in the Jeep and just threw the medicine to the patients. In her clinic the nurses put the ointment on their sores and medicine into their hands and gave them milk powder to supplement their meager diet. The hands that dispensed these things are truly different. They are hands of love. You will recall that

13

once a leper came to Jesus and said, "If you wish, you can heal me." Jesus replied, "I do wish," and touched him. To touch a leper is a sure sign of love. The government can employ doctors and nurses to give the treatment needed, but they cannot buy Christian love. That is found only in those who received it from God.

Ruth Eveland
Missionary India 1925-1965
(Methodist Episcopal Church; The Methodist Church)
(Submitted 1975)

An Experience in Puerto Rico

When I arrived in Puerto Rico in August 1929 the director of the Robinson School was delighted that I could not speak one word of Spanish nor understand it either. The theory was that the children would have to learn English fast. So after I had been there a week several of us teachers went to find a movie made here with Spanish interpretation beneath the picture. I was grateful that they were helped that much.

Afterwards, because this was the last time for a year that we could all get away together, someone suggested that we have some ice cream to finish our good time away from the children. I was the last one to order, and told the waiter that I would like a Hot Fudge Sundae best. But he said, "It isn't Sunday, It's Saturday." Everyone except me and the waiter had a good laugh. Then Mercedes explained to him what I meant. He understood perfectly then, and everybody but the two of us had a good laugh.

Puerto Rico 1929-1938;
Various USA appointments 1944-1960
(Methodist Episcopal Church, The Methodist Church)
(Submitted 1975)

A Letter That Changed the Tide of My Life

It was early summer in 1924. I was working in a "Neighborhood House" in Dupont, a shabby little mining town between Scranton and Wilkes-Barre, Pennsylvania. In 1921 I had graduated from Missionary Training Institute at Nyack-on-Hudson and had expected to be sent to Africa. But after my mother's death it seemed to be my duty to remain at home to care for the younger members of the family. So I regretfully gave up the hope of going to the mission field.

Circumstances changed unexpectedly, and I was free to seek employment outside our farm home, which had been sold. Positions in a YWCA camp for the summer, and for the winter Christian Education in a public school near Gettysburg were offered, but for some reason I could not decide to accept either one. I thought, I reasoned, and prayed about it, but seemed unable to say "Yes" or "No."

A friend on the YWCA Board was waiting for my decision at noon on Monday, "my day off." I sat alone, watching the clock, wondering what I should say when I telephoned her. Just before twelve o'clock, I started across the room. At that moment I saw the postman coming. I said to myself, "I'll wait and see what the mail has brought."

There was a letter from the Student Volunteer Movement, asking if I would go to China to teach in the Kuling American School. I called my friend and told her that I would not be available as a counselor at camp. In surprise and almost unbelief, she asked, "Why, Jane, why not?" Calmly I answered "Because I am going to China."

In three weeks I was ready to sail from San Francisco. God had guided and answered my prayer, just in time. Forty years were spent in China, Brazil and Japan. I think of that day as one of the most significant of my whole life. I thank God for his goodness and mercy which have followed all the days thereafter.

Jenny Lind
Missionary
China 1924-1927. 1929-1940, 1948-50;
Brazil 1944-46? : Japan 1950-61
(Methodist Episcopal Church, The Methodist Church)
(Submitted 1975)

Disaster Ministry, Buffalo Creek, West Virginia
1972-1974

Working in a disaster ministry was an in-depth experience for me. Even my call to go there meant a time of evaluation. What was my preparation for such a ministry? I could look back and see how God had brought me to "such a time as this" – experiences in coal fields, in Harlan County, Kentucky, floods, in West Virginia, in community development counseling and work with youth. The call was clear.

A mine dam burst on an early February morning. Sixteen communities were almost totally destroyed; over 100 died; more than 600 families were displaced. Mobile home communities were set up without regard to former neighborhoods. People worked out their grief among strangers. Wesley Community Center was the one meeting place left standing. It became the umbrella for many types of ministry. Pastoral counseling through the Church of the Brethren, the Presbyterian, the United Methodist churches became the heart of our effort. Wesley House served Mennonites, the American Friends Service, The Governor's Disaster Committee and community groups.

A group of women who just wanted to "do their own thing" to bring about their own healing made a quilt. I called it a THERAPY QUILT. On each block was drawn and embroidered some building representing a phase of disaster recovery. It was set up at Wesley Center for quilting. Many visitors to the valley felt it had an almost supernatural quality, as though it came alive and spoke of suffering and the spirit of the people. The quilt went to the fair. A thousand dollars was offered for it, but this quilt could not be sold at any price.

Later I was called back for the dedication and hanging of the THERAPY QUILT on the auditorium wall. A big celebration took place. Thankfulness to God and to those who helped with rehabilitation was freely given. "God works in a mysterious way, His wonders to perform." A quilt had become a symbol of God's caring love.

Jennie D. Flood
Deaconess USA 1943-1976
(The Methodist Church; United Methodist Church)
(Submitted 1981)

Seiwa College, Nishinomiya, Japan and My Visit to China

Seiwa College celebrated its 100th Anniversary the first week in November. Sallie Carrell and I, having taught there for many years, went back for the occasion. More than 1000 graduates and many other people were there. It was a joy to see them and participate in the activities.

When I first went to Seiwa 30 years ago (I could no longer serve in China because of the Communist takeover) there were about 80 students, all preparing for Christian service. Some were kindergarten teachers and some were Christian Education workers. Now Seiwa is a senior college, with an extra year for specialized work for those who want it. There has always been a kindergarten at the college where students do their practice teaching. Christian Education students help in church and social service work. The college has continued to grow in size and services. There are more than 900 students. Several buildings were erected during my years there, and some since then. It is a fine, well-equipped college. Seiwa graduates are serving in a number of places, some outside Japan.

Following the Anniversary, Sallie and I visited some of our former students in various places and saw some of the fine work they are doing. Graduates gathered in Kyoto, Hiroshima and Tokyo for meetings and fellowship with us. Traveling, sightseeing, participating in meetings, and in various activities with graduates and other friends filled our days with joy. Our month in Japan aroused happy memories and gave us the opportunity to see many friends.

Following my visit to Japan, Sallie Carroll and I spent a week in Shanghai, China where I served from 1929 until after the communists took over in 1949. Mrs. Weng, a graduate of McTyeire School (now Municipal High School 3), where I taught, and Miss Hsu, our CITS guide, met us at the airport and took us to the Peace Hotel. Miss Sih Tsung, a teacher and good friend, greeted us and helped make plans for our visit. She planned a tea at the school for teachers and students whom I knew years ago. Many memories were aroused as we visited and toured the campus, including the house where I had lived!

Each morning before we started on our sight-seeing trip, groups of friends came. It was a joy having time with them. Our guide took Sallie and me to interesting places where we saw people working in factories, carving ivory, working with jade, etc. At the Children's Palace, groups were playing violins and other instruments, practicing plays, embroidering, painting, making dolls and puppets, repairing radios.

On Sunday morning we attended the 10:30 service at Moen Dang (formerly Moore Memorial Church), where a 6:30 and an 8:30 service, as well as the 10:30 service, are held. There are about 2000 people at each service; 1200 in the sanctuary and others in the classrooms. About one-fourth of them are thirty years of age or under. Miss Kiang Kwe-yun and the Rev. Z.S. Zia, friends for many years, sat with us.

The Shanghai population, seven million, is staggering; streets are crowded with bicycles, masses of friendly people spend time walking; and a few buses and cars join the traffic, patrolled by officers in white uniforms, located in elevated control towers situated on the sidewalks. I am grateful for my visit to China.

Pearle McCain

Missionary

Sue Bennett College, London, KY 1925-1929;

China 1929-1942? , 1946-1949;

Japan 1951-1971

(Methodist Episcopal Church, South;

The Methodist Church; United Methodist Church)

(Submitted 1981)

Back to Japan After 18 Years

Ayoma Women's Junior College, where I taught my last six years in Japan, extended me an urgent invitation to attend their 35th Anniversary Celebration on November 8. I arrived in Osaka on November 4, my first visit to Japan since I retired 18 years ago. On November 7, I flew to Tokyo. To my surprise, seven members of my former Graduates' English Bible Class met me at the airport, and those girls, now mature women, transported me wherever I wished to go while I was there.

The day of the celebration was interesting and informative and I saw several teachers and students of 18 years ago. The College, which had formerly been housed in a frame building, now had modern buildings accommodating nearly 2000 students. On this same campus is now located the University, senior and junior high and primary schools, and a kindergarten under Methodist auspices.

I had one full day with the above mentioned "girls," in a home, a never-to-be-forgotten day, and had the pleasure of being present at a missionary get-together one night.

The Chancellor of the Ayoma University gave a dinner in my honor at one of the hotels where special Japanese and missionary friends were present. Before I left, the college presented me with a gift of $150, plus a plane ticket to Hiroshima, my next destination. I was overwhelmed with it all. . .so unexpected when I left for my visit to Japan. All of my "girls" were at the airport to wave goodbye as I left for Hiroshima.

Three and one-half days in Hiroshima gave me the opportunity to visit the Hiroshima Jo Gakuin (junior and senior high schools and college), and the Gaines Memorial Kindergarten, as well as to see friends of former years, including a missionary, Doris Hartman. I had an unexpected joy when a retired minister from Kure, where I worked my first twelve years in Japan, brought two elderly women from the church there to see me…he is 78 and the women are 83 and 88. What a happy time we had reliving those days of the 1920s and early 1930s.

My last and final stop was Kobe, where I spent five years immediately after the war. I rode the 'Bullet," Japan's fastest train, from Hiroshima to Kobe, and got a good look at the countryside. It was quite different from that of former days. In Kobe I was conveniently located where friends from Kyoto, Osaka and neighboring towns could come to visit. What a joy to see them all! I spent a day with a couple for whom I had arranged their marriage more than fifty years ago. We had kept in touch through all these years. And ten members of a Women's Bible Class during my years in Kobe came one day. Then we had another afternoon together in one of the homes. (Fortunately my command of the Japanese language came back to me even though I have rarely used it since retirement.) On Sunday I attended the church where I had been a member, briefly visited the two schools where I had taught, and walked the old familiar streets again. A nostalgic time!

I cannot adequately express the deep satisfaction which was mine in seeing so many dear friends of long ago. It added to my joy to see how happy they were to see me again! We talked and laughed and shed tears of joy as we thanked God for making it possible for us to meet again. I returned to the United States after my two and one half week visit, feeling that God had truly given His approval for the trip.

Mary Searcy
Missionary

Japan 1920-1941, 1947-1952, 1956-1961
(Methodist Episcopal Church, South; The Methodist Church)
(Submitted 1981)

Love

In the summer of 1954 Holding Institute, Loredo, Texas—a school grades 1 through 12 plus a Special Department for beginners in the study of English—was destroyed by fire.

The Executive Secretary from the Woman's Division of Christian Service came. The consensus was that the school MUST CONTINUE ON THE BORDER OF MEXICO. It would continue in 1954-55 by teaching the Special Department in rooms loaned by the Junior College until a new building was erected. Other employed staff were offered positions elsewhere.

Then the Secretary asked if there was anything that Ura Leveridge could do if she remained here. Why such a question about one who had served as a deaconess in many capacities for 30 years? Ura had a hearing problem which now made it impossible to function in the classroom, but she would be housemother for 15 boys. Did she spurn this offer because of her Master's degrees in both English and Bible? No! It gave her the opportunity to continue serving students whom she loved.

On the new campus was a cottage where she and the boys lived. Here she prepared two meals a day for them and helped them with English and other problems. As she did this, she also watched new buildings rise, one by one. At the end of the year, a Roman Catholic boy likened her to a saint! What greater tribute could he have given?

There are three things that last forever: Faith, Hope and Love, but the greatest of them all—is LOVE. I Corinthians 13:13 (NEB).

Mary E. Glendinning
Deaconess USA
1926-1954—Holding Institute (and study);
1954-1957—Browning Home
1957-1962--Mather Academy
1963-1966, volunteer, Holding Institute
(Methodist Episcopal Church, South; The Methodist Church)
(Submitted 1982)

A Spiritual Experience

While working in Kentucky a friend and I one day drove past Mrs. Eva Alexander's home. I remarked that Eva would become a Christian someday soon. The friend said she hoped she would, but that I did not know the kind of life she was living. Later I told Eva I would conduct a prayer service in her home any time she wished. A date was set. When the day came two girls from Wilson College were spending the weekend with me. I told them if they went with me it would be a routine meeting, but if they did not go, Eva's life would be changed that afternoon. They stayed in my apartment.

About a dozen people gathered for the service. After songs, prayer and the message, I gave the invitation and waited, knowing there would be a response. From the top of a side wall there emerged an influence that moved across the room and filled it. There was no noise or wind as on the Day of Pentecost, but it was a manifestation of the power of the Holy Spirit. Eva, her teenage daughter and four other teenage girls made their professions of faith. They joined the church on Easter Day.

Cora Lee Glenn
Deaconess, Rural Worker USA 1920-1970
(Methodist Episcopal Church, South;
The Methodist Church; United Methodist Church)

(Submitted 1982)

When I was appointed to be hostess

I remember many things about the two years when I was appointed to be hostess to "ALL INCOMING AND OUTGOING MISSIONARIES" of the newly organized Board of Missions (1940). It was a rich and rewarding experience as I greeted many new friends coming into the Port of New York from their fields of service.

When the United States declared war, most missionaries were recalled and they came home on ships of all sizes. Plane travel was a rare thing in those days!

I remember meeting a family with four children who had been zig-zagging on a ship for about eight weeks, trying to evade the feared German submarines that prowled the sea lanes. After clearing at Customs, I managed to get the family and I into one taxi and suggested we go to the offices of the Board. But not so! The mother wanted to have her hair done and the father wanted nothing more than to get to the hotel where space had been reserved.

But first of all, everyone wanted a meal in an American restaurant. We went to the lovely dining room of the famous John Wanamaker's Department Store on lower Broadway (long since gone),during which time the four-year-old child managed to decorate herself with chocolate ice cream! I took the mother to the beauty shop and the father to the hotel. Then the four children and I went to the Visitors' Lounge at the Board offices, where I spent the rest of the day baby-sitting.

Alice E. Murdock
Board of Missions Staff 1941-52
(The Methodist Church)
(Submitted 1982)

An Experience in Cuba

When serving as principal of the Agricultural School while the missionary principal and his wife were on furlough, our oldest student in the school, a late teenager, was of such exemplary character that he was helping the professor in charge of the boys and leading them in a fine way. One day he began working in the school shop without the goggles they were supposed to wear, and a piece of metal flew into his eyes. They brought him to me in great pain, so the nurse and I decided to  get him to the hospital in Preston, the sugar-mill town near the school. They kept him one night but early the next morning sent him back to the school with the message to send him at once to the city of Santiago, Cuba. There they removed the eye and replaced it with an artificial one.

After a month he returned to school. He was a completely different person—surly, moody, indifferent, irritable with the boys. I sent for him to come to my house, where I faced him in the living room. I told him we were puzzled about the change in him and asked why he had become like that. He burst out, saying, "I'm not any good anymore. I'm not a whole person. I have only one eye!"

I sent up a silent plea to God to help me, and said quietly, "Roberto, since I was nine years old I have had only one eye to work with. If I try to use it, the vision crosses the vision in the other eye. So, I worked about twenty years in Cuba as a missionary using only one eye. You can get along alright with one eye, do whatever work you decide to do. So be thankful you have your sight and go ahead as if you had two eyes."

He sat there looking at me for a minute, then jumped up and came over to give me a hug, and said, "Thank you, Miss Gaby." His face lighted up as he left.

I had always thought of my unusable eye as a cross to be borne. Now I sat there a minute to thank God that I had only one eye, so I could help Roberto see that he need not feel inferior because he had only one eye.

An Experience in Cuba (2)

I was serving as principal of Buenavista School in Havana while the regular principal was on furlough. One day the secretary came running back from an errand I had sent her on, white-faced and trembling and said, "Miss Gaby, come upstairs quickly! Maria is trying to throw herself down from the balcony!"

I jumped up, ran out of the office and up the stairs two at a time, and went to the door opening out onto the balcony. Maria was the spoiled twelve-year-old daughter of a man

23

who owned three tobacco factories. He and his wife gave her whatever she wanted and let her do whatever she wanted to. I stood in the doorway, scared and shaky, and said in an authoritative voice, "Maria, get down from there!"

She turned her head, saw it was I, and slowly climbed down off the railing and came to me. She had painted her face, put on her school uniform backwards, and rumpled up her hair. She looked frightful. I ordered the other girls who had been holding her to keep her from jumping to go to their rooms, and putting my arm around Maria, I led her back to her room and asked her to wash her face, comb her hair, put on a robe, and then we would talk. In a few minutes she came out, looking more like herself, but she had been crying. Sitting by her, I asked her to tell me why she was trying to throw herself down from the balcony.

She began crying, and said her father didn't love her anymore. She showed me a telegram from him that said he could not come for her that Friday, that a letter would follow. It was a long weekend because of a holiday, and all the other girls were going home. I tried to reason with her, telling her that her father really could not come to get her, and she would find out why when she got his letter. But she shook her head, saying that he did not love her and she was going to kill herself. Finally, I got her to promise that she would wait for the letter. It came the next morning, special delivery. She opened it with shaking hands, read it, then came to give it to me. It said he and her mother were under house arrest by a group of communists who had taken over the factory and he would come to the school as soon as they were free. I said to Maria, "You see, Maria, why he could not come. Your father does love you!"

She put her hand on my shoulder, cried, then turned and went to her room, smiling through her tears.

Frances Gaby
Missionary Cuba 1928-1960
Cuban Refugee work 6 years
(Methodist Episcopal Church, South, The Methodist Church)
(Submitted 1984)

The Tiger Who Would Look At His Aunt

 It was our last day in the hill station of Pachmarhi, where my friend and I had been vacationing. Tomorrow we would drive back to our stations. We decided on one last drive out to the highest hill in Central India the Fortress of the Sun. I had twisted my ankle the day before, so I would walk about with Dusty, our kitten, while Miriam would walk to the very top, accompanied by the cook and the driver. I started up the path with them, followed by Dusty, who stopped often to investigate interesting smells or chase insects. Every now and then he would meow and hurry to catch up until he found something else to investigate. Once as he moved I turned back to encourage him to come on, and I found a movement through the tall grass. Good gracious! Could it be a tiger sitting on its haunches? I bent to one side for a better look; so did the tiger. The cat meowed, the tiger tried to locate the maker of the sound. Could it really be a tiger at nine o'clock on this bright rain-washed day? Going back, I scooped up the protesting Dusty and carried him back to the car and locked him in it. Then I smelled the tiger! He had followed us to the other side of the small ridge. Try as I would, I couldn't see him this time among the bushes.

Some road workers arrived from town and passed me as they went up the hill. I asked whether there were tigers around these days. They said, "Of course" – and kept on climbing. An older man came along. He stopped to talk. I repeated my question and was told that a young male tiger had been coming every day to sun himself on the large flat rock near which a little stream flowed. I told him I had seen him, I thought. Still I could hardly believe it.

When Miriam came back I told her I had probably seen a tiger. She exclaimed, "Down here in broad daylight! You would have the luck!"

I asked her and the two men to walk back with me to the spot. There was nothing there but some flattened grass where he had been lying, when Dusty's meow had brought him to a sitting position and to my attention. So Dusty was responsible for what I had seen. The man said that after all, the tiger wanted to see his aunt. In Indian folklore the cat is the aunt of the tiger!

Louise Campbell
Missionary India 1931-1983 (stayed on after retirement at the request of the Indian Conference)
(The Methodist Church; United Methodist Church)
(Submitted 1984)

Christ in Korea

 Koreans have a great civilization which dates back to 4000 B.C. They believed in one God who was benign, but were more concerned about buying off the evil spirit which brought troubles of all kinds. The Sorceress was consulted, especially at the beginning of a new year. Catholiv Christians came into uninvited and officially unwanted. Because officially unwelcomed, persecution resulted for those who taught the "pernicious Jesus doctrine." Government had been for the protection of the ruling class, and to have the lower and middle classes cared for was presumably not pleasing.

Through Horace Allen, an M.D. to the Emperor of the Ye Dynasty, Protestant missionaries were given a special invitation to come and share Western medicine and civilization in 1885, one hundred years ago, Now, in 1984, one in every four are Christian! In Confucian ethics, women were kept sequestered in the home, and no girl or woman was to be seen by a male of another family after the age of 7. Now girls began to go to school! As late as 1914 a girl was considered a bold, bad girl if she went to college. But, go they did, and when Korea gained independence at the end of World War II, Dr. Helen Kim was asked by the President to set up the educational system of the country, and she did. Ewha University, the world's largest university for women, has graduated other important leaders. Among them is Ye Tae-Young, an important lawyer. Cho Wha-Soon, another woman of influence, became a worker in a textile factory where the conditions and wages were disgraceful. She tried to change conditions for the better and suffered for it; she was toppled down a stairway and trampled on. The President promises corporations cheap labor and does not approve of change.

Even while I was still serving in Korea, they were already sending missionaries to other countries. At the June International Missions Seminar, Bishop Suh said, "Korea has a world-wide mission!"

Esther Hulbert
Missionary Korea 1923-1939; Cuba 1942-1960
Methodist Episcopal Church; The Methodist Church)

(Submitted 1984)

A Trip to Korea

What does one expect to see after an absence of nineteen years? I was lost in Seoul. In the business sections of the city the streets and sidewalks were well filled. In some places I counted six lanes of traffic in each direction!

The economic situation of individuals had improved to a great extent. In several towns that I had known the church had been rebuilt and was about three times the former size. At one place north of Seoul, I noticed a number of irregular stones, six or eight feet tall lining the road. Why? To block the road south in case South Korea is attacked from the north.

The church is growing in Korea while the inhabitants face an uncertain future. I understand a number of Koreans have gone as missionaries to other countries. My joy in returning was seeing people I had known. One man, who was a child in 1925 when we first met, spoke to me. The Presiding Bishop at the Methodist Centennial is someone with whom I had worked on the district level when he was District Superintendent. There was the joy of seeing many Koreans I had known through the years, of being with missionary friends again and having some time with a step-son and his family,

Eulene Weems
Korea 1925-1940; 1953-1965
(Methodist Episcopal Church, South; The Methodist Church)

(Submitted 1984)

Eager Students

Among the most rewarding experiences during my years in India was the Village Women's Institutes. The village pastors of the particular area would help in selecting the women of younger ages who showed ability to take responsibility in the local church. They arrived with bedding, clothes, grain donations on their heads—and their babies too small to leave with the father on their hips.

They were free to sit together with uncovered faces and to participate, as there were no men in our group. Such freedom! They learned Bible verses and stories, loved to sing, to play together, and prepare colored pictures to put on their dirt walls!

At one institute an older woman brought two younger women who could not have come alone. Sambai became very interested in what the women were learning and doing. A series of flannelgraph lessons on the Life of Christ leading up to His death and resurrection deeply touched her as we talked about His suffering and death on the cross, Sambai was the first to answer the question, "Why is the cross empty now?"

She said, "Jesus was wounded; He died and the men buried Him. Then he got well, and came out of the grave. Now He lives in my heart!"

These women were illiterate in "letters," but being eager pupils, they became excellent "students"! Their husbands would tell the pastors how different the women were when they returned home and with great interest asked when they would be called again"

Florence Palmer
Missionary India 1930-1958, 1964-1968
Board Staff: Executive Secretary for Women's
Work in India, Pakistan and Nepal 1959-1963
(Methodist Episcopal Church, The Methodist Church)
(Submitted 1985)

A Complex Dilemma

Emotionally upset, Mrs. Woody* with her two boys and a girl (ages 12, 10, and 8) came to Wesley House Centers** and told the director of her dilemma. After completing a 12-month minor offence limited prison term, Mr. Woody was coming home in three days. He had no job; their money was all gone; utilities were turned off; eviction notice received. Mrs. Woody anxiously asked, "What can we do? Where can we live? How can we get food with no money?"

She was assured that Wesley House would help her as she discussed plans and resources with the director. Before discussions began, the mother and the director prayed together for God's guidance in coping with her family problems. After contacting possible resources and relatives, the Director/Minister of the Children's Home—with parents, children, and some United Methodist Women***--set a plan in motion.

The Methodist Children's Home admitted the children for a temporary stay; relatives provided a place for the parents to stay; a part-time job provided Mr. Woody with means to rent a two-room apartment. Eventually he secured a job with the city's Public Health Authorities. The family was now reunited and moved into an apartment in the Housing Project. Soon Mr. Woody's salary exceeded the maximum eligibility salary for living in the public facility. The good fortune enabled the parents to rent a one-family dwelling. Later personal contact showed the family was comfortably situated and doing well—a good reason for rejoicing!

Because of the cooperative efforts of the Methodist institutions and loving, caring people, a troubled family avoided the tragic disintegration which so often occurs in similar situations. Wesley House Centers, according to its purpose, helped a family in need. When committed, dedicated people join forces to meet a need, we know that God's Redemptive Love is still at work in our troubled world!

*Not his real name
**Atlanta, Georgia
***This event occurred sometime between 1950 and 1962; this would have been the Woman's Society of Christian Service.

Rosamond Johnson
Deaconess USA 1937-1973
(Methodist Episcopal Church, South; The Methodist Church)
(Submitted 1985)

China

Miss Susan Armstrong, teacher in a boys' school in Foochow, told about a pupil who came to her near Christmas time in much distress. He was to be married the following day, but could not afford a veil for his bride. (In Kutien we always kept two veils on hand—renting one for a dollar and the other, of better material, for two dollars.) The groom could not even afford a feast (an unusual circumstance) so the wedding was to be quiet and private, but the bride must be veiled. Susan knew silk or rayon would be too expensive and cotton would not look right. So she bought several yards of white mosquito netting and dyed it a lovely pink. Then, as she fitted and sewed it—the bride not being present—the groom modeled. By mid afternoon the veil was finished and pronounced beautiful by everyone who saw it.

Marion Holmes
Missionary to China, Malaysia, Sarawak
1931-1950, 1957-1964
(Methodist Episcopal Church)
(Submitted 1987)

Peru

A father brought his little boy to our school, saying "You can do more for him than I can."

Earthquakes were fairly common in Peru and this little boy of five or six was very frightened and started to cry.

"You must not cry," we said to him, "for Jesus is here to care for you."

"But I don't see Him anywhere," said the little fellow. So we showed him a picture of Jesus and that satisfied him. This little fellow is now grown up. The last we knew of him he was studying in Spain.

Sameramis (Sammy) Kutz
Missionary to Peru, Chile 1936?-1964
(Methodist Episcopal Church, The Methodist Church)
(Submitted 1987)

Thailand

For two years at the beginning of retirement, I worked at a Christian University in Chiang Mai, Thailand—about 500 miles north of Bangkok. This is the only school in Thailand offering students a degree in music. For months a choir of thirty Thai young people, plus two of the music professors (one an American and the other an Indian), together with an orchestra of thirteen (ten Thai students and three American instructors), practiced, in English, Handel's *Messiah*. One evening in early December the cantata was presented in the University chapel to a packed audience of more than 500 students. What a thrill! In that Buddhist country where less than 1% of the population is Christian—to see and feel the reaction as all rose for the Hallelujah Chorus! Granted, some did not know why they stood for that particular portion—but the impact on the entire congregation was tremendous--quite a Christian testimony. This rendition of the *Messiah* also made history. It was the first time in Thailand that the Messiah had been presented with a predominantly Thai cast.

Lucy Rowe
Missionary to Nigeria 1946-1952, 1957-1963;
Sarawak, Malaysia 1964-1968
(Evangelical Church   Evangelical United Brethren Church
United Methodist Church)
(Submitted 1987)

Go Tell It On the Mountains

Why would a deaconess who had had most challenging appointments, and was within twelve years of retirement, want to be a minister? My answer is that I wanted to share the Christian message in regular specific words as well as deeds. My younger ministerial friends encouraged me.

To present Christ I needed to get to know Him and all about Him in greater depth. So I took a furlough and went to Drew Seminary for a year. My first appointment was a charge of two active churches.

I had never had a desire to go to the Holy Land, but this appealed to me as a good way to know Him better. Soon the parishioners were all excited about such a trip for me, making me promise to tell all about it on my return. Although they did not pay for the trip, those "Happy Journey" cards were reinforced with money gifts of various denominations.

The tour was called "In the Steps of the Master," and none before or since have equaled it, in my mind. We were away three weeks and traveled some familiar scenes and some untraveled territory, as from Damascus to Antioch where followers of Christ were first called Christians.

One of the high points of the trip was Christmas Eve and Christmas Day in Shepherds Field and in Bethlehem. With great expectations we left Jerusalem by bus on Christmas Eve. What a lovely night! When we reached the gate at Shepherds Field we disembarked and made our way to the cave area. There a section had been prepared for our gathering for worship. The stars were shining, the sheep bleating and people had come from "all corners of the globe." I even saw my Old Testament teacher from Drew. Then the singing began—singing in two or more languages. The scriptures and messages were also in more than one tongue. Of course our minds were drawn to that night when the angels sang "Glory to God in the Highest."

After the service we were invited into the cave for meat and bread. Then, on the way to the bus we saw a United Nations vehicle and two young girls helping those who had taken ill. This further reminded us that this was a world Christian gathering.

The next day we made our way to Bethlehem. In long lines leading into the Church of the Nativity people were waiting. To this line were added, one following the other, choir boys, scouts, soldiers and men on horses. Then all of us waited for the archbishop, recognized in the distance by his red hat. We followed him into the church, then went down the stairs to the manger room. Of course it did not fit our own conception, but it was not difficult to feel the importance of the place.

Before I left I wondered what I would take the Baby. The answer came, "Why, of course, a blanket." When I arrived I wondered what I would do with it. The voice spoke again, "Giving to these little ones is the same as giving to Me." I gave the blanket to a refugee.

All during my trip I was taking pictures and composing script. I was received joyfully on my return. Certainly my pictures and words about the entire trip were experienced with meaning. Shorter scripts followed, one of which was "The Messages of the Mountains."

Not only was my life, and those of the parishioners, enriched this one year, but in all the years that followed.

Margaret Marshall

Deaconess USA 1927-1960

Ordained minister 1960-West Virginia
(Methodist Episcopal Church, South;
The Methodist Church, United Methodist Church)

(Submitted 1990)

News from Zaire

It was a happy day in March for Annimae White and me when two of our Zaire colleagues, Douglas Crowder and his wife Elaine, came to see us. Doug was the missionary builder for the new school building of "Lycee Mama Tola" at Lodja, the school in which I was involved.*

As we sat at the dinner table one day it was almost like a reunion, as there were present six out of eight of us who attended the dedication of that building last May. Yes, there we were: the Crowders; Jack Miner, a volunteer, spent two terms of three months each helping with the construction; Renie, his wife, with whom I traveled to the dedication; and Rev. Bob Boggan, Conference Mission Secretary, who also attended the dedication. Special guests, friends of the Crowders in Zaire, were Dr. and Mrs. Robert Turk of Asheville.

The Crowders have traveled 10,000 miles since January, speaking in churches. While in Asheville they and Jack spoke in two United Methodist Churches, Groce and Berry Temple.

It was a joy to get news of the church in Zaire from the Crowders and to discuss with them projects and plans for the future in the Central Zaire Conference.

*The school was named in honor of Lorena—"Mama Tola."

Lorena Kelly
Deaconess U.S. 1932-1935
Missionary Congo (Zaire) 1935-1970
(Methodist Episcopal Church, South,
The Methodist Church, United Methodist Church)
(Submitted 1991)

Return Home to Mozambique

It was indeed a privilege to visit many friends in Mozambique for nine weeks, after having made my home there for thirty-nine years. What a wonderful family— former students and colleagues. How thrilling it was to visit first hand the tremendous expansion of the church in the suburbs, far into the north where, in colonial days the Portuguese would not permit us to expand.

Rev. Feliz Navess was an enthusiastic youth at Cambine, witnessing to others when in the army, and whenever time permitted his worshiping on Sundays, he would gather the other youth together. Now he is an ordained pastor way up north. He sent me pictures of his well-organized congregation. Plans are made for building a church so they will have a place to meet! His joy in the presence of Christ leading his life is contagious.

Former students are now capably leading in positions of influence in the community and government, maintaining their Christian witness.

There is still tension, knowing the Resistance Movement may attack at any moment, but in spite of this the Church is growing! Desolate, bereaved, hungry, but grateful to be alive— one finds warm love, caring, sharing of meager supplies and over-crowded dwellings; but the love of Christ is magnifying the little to be sufficient.

Dialogue is being carried on with leaders of the Resistance Movement <u>when</u> they consent but, unfortunately, there are wealthy foreigners who back them with funds and keep them going with mistaken and wrong counsel.

Thanks be to God for the strong and faithful courage of Christians who are leading the churches into caring ministry, and bringing many who had lost all hope to Christ and to His salvation. We do have a vision of PEACE in Mozambique!

Mary Jean Tennant
Missionary Mozambique 1948-1989
(The Methodist Church, United Methodist Church)
(Submitted 1991)

A Miracle at Work

In May 1992 I saw a miracle at work in Korea.

In 1986 I had the joy of attending the centenary celebrations of the founding of the largest women's university in the world—Ewha University in Seoul, Korea. It was at Ewha and Yonsei Universities that God had given me the opportunity, for almost twenty years, to help train general surgeons at their medical colleges.

We were also, as United Methodist missionaries, related to the Inchon Christian Hospital, where Dr. Suk Bong Kang had been superintendent and leader since 1952.

At the time of the Ewha celebration I was invited by Dr. Suk Bong Kang to come to Inchon in 1992 for their 40th anniversary celebration.

Since 1986 word came that Dr. Kang had gastric cancer surgery. Later he had hepatic cancer. How could there be a 40th anniversary celebration? Last Christmas a letter stated "I've had a rough time. With God's love and grace, chemotherapy and the new treatment, I am at work, planning for the May celebration, and I expect you."

What a joy to see him still dreaming and planning for the future, and to see how a little missionary house, once a small clinic, is now a large medical center with a School of Nursing and Allied Sciences.

It was a joy to worship in a service with a congregation of over 3,000 and to know that that church is sending out five missionaries.

It was a joy to see former students—now surgeons, a medical school dean and a hospital superintendent..

Korea is one people, one language. With God's help soon it will become again one country.

Roberta G. Rice, M.D.
Missionary Korea 1956-1975
(The Methodist Church, United Methodist Church)
(Submitted1992)

A Star of Love and Peace in a Troubled Land

God enabled me to be in the Holy Land, in the Occupied West Bank, for five weeks this winter, as a "Volunteer in Mission." Direct involvement in the tension and problems there, especially the Hebron Massacre and its aftermath, plus the faithful and loving witness of the persons at the Bethlehem Bible College, made the new Testament seem incredibly timely, as though Paul, Peter and John were writing for today,

Founded in 1979, Bethlehem Bible College shines as "A Star of Love and Peace in a Troubled Land" as it prepares Palestinian Christians for the ministry, orients foreign visitors to the reality of West Bank life, strives to be faithful to the Prince of Peace in a ministry of reconciliation among Muslims, Jews and Christians; and serves spiritually and materially in the two refugee camps and in the orphanages in the area.

Christian biblical and theological materials are very limited in Arabic, the students' first language, so research must be done in English. My task was to classify the nearly 3,000 books in these fields more concisely and set up cross-reference subject matter themes which enable the students to find exactly what they are looking for. Later, all this will be put on a computer.

Bethlehem Bible College is an approved Advance Special mission project. Alex Awad and his family will return to Palestine in August to serve as United Methodist missionaries. Please continue to pray for the witness of the Bible College and for peace in the Holy Land.

Patricia Riddell
Volunteer in Mission to Palestine 1994
Retired missionary to Latin America:
Short-term missionary to Argentina 1957-1959,
Woman's Division missionary to Peru 1960-1973,
Mexico , 1973-1992, (with eight months in Sierra Leone & Liberia in 1979, working on curriculum for the Sunday Schools);
retired from Mexico 1992.
1992, 1993 Mission Interpreter in Residence in Southeastern Jurisdiction UMC
(The Methodist Church, United Methodist Church)
(Submitted 1994)

Learnings from Nicaragua

I recently spent two months in Nicaragua, and I learned more than I wanted to know about this small country now. In eight short years, it has come to exceed Haiti in its indices of poverty. Everywhere one looks, there are indications of this. The infrastructure has deteriorated badly. People seek any means possible by which to make enough money to put food on the table. Unemployment is now 70%. The systems of education, health care and social services are in   shambles. Education has been privatized, which means that students pay for every expense, and they pay to attend the schools. When the new government came in 1990 the first things eliminated were the preschools and adult education. There was a quick and thorough revision of textbooks at every level to eliminate  references to the *campesinos* and/or the Revolution. In the small village of seventy families where our Witness for Peace group spent five nights, we held several meetings in the small school. It broke my heart to become acquainted with Lisette and her cousin who are already beyond the third grade, as far as the school goes. These intelligent young people will have no further education, because they cannot afford the transportation to attend school in another village. The Health system, too, has been privatized. Government doctors receive $56.00 a month. For the last three months doctors have been on strike, and many communities are left with no health care beyond that of the nurses. A woman doctor, covering five small villages because she was the only one who served while on strike, talked with us.   When one of our group asked if they could initiate such and such a procedure, the doctor said, "We cannot make the decisions that would benefit our people. We are at the mercy of our national debt, and the structural adjustment policies of the World Bank and the International Monetary Fund." These structural adjustment policies, the second round, will now privatize both water and electricity.

Some of you are aware that I came home exhausted—really wiped out. A part of this was the depression that envelops one when you live day after day with an awareness of such a difficult situation.

In the midst of this stands the Christian Base Community where I was privileged to teach English again, and to attend the "People's Mass" whenever I was in town on Sunday night. I should like to share the English translation of the chorus of the Entrance song of the Mass, and then the Credo of that Mass, both a part of each service. First the chorus:

You are the God of the poor,
The human and simple God,
The God who sweats in the street,
The God with the weather-beaten face.
That is why I can talk with you
The way I talk with my people.
Because you are God the worker,
And Christ was a worker, too.

And the Credo:

Chorus:

I believe in you, Architect, Engineer,
Artisan, Carpenter, Mason and Assembler,
I believe in you, Constructor of thought,
Of music and the wind, of peace and love.

I firmly believe, God, that from your generous mind
All this world was born; that from your artist's hand
As a primitivist painter, beauty flourished;
The stars and the moon, the little homes, the lagoons,
The small ships navigating down the river toward the sea,
The immense coffee plantations, the white cotton fields,
And the forest that has been mutilated by the criminal hatchet.
I believe in you, Companion, Human Christ, Worker Christ,
    Conqueror of death;
With your immense sacrifice you begat the new person
    for freedom.
You are resurrected in every arm that is raised
To defend the people from the dominating exploiter;
I believe in your resurrection.

(Author and translator unknown.)

Helene R. Hill
Deaconess USA 1950-1986
(The Methodist Church, United Methodist Church)
(Submitted 1997)

Volunteering in Armenia

Six members of Oakley United Methodist Church [in Asheville] visited Armenia from July 18 to August 4, 1998. Pat Riddell and Frances Major, residents of Brooks-Howell, were members of the team. Our purpose was to share our Christian Education methods with the Armenians. During the first week we divided into two teams and conducted Daily Bible School in cooperation with the Armenian Evangelical Church as arranged by our Agape staff. In these four schools  we reached more than 300 children. Three of the team were in Yerevan, the large capital city, and three of us went to Gyumri, a two-hour drive from Yerevan. Gyumri was the epicenter of the 1988 earthquake and there are still both visible and invisible signs of that earthquake that killed more than 25,000 people and greatly crippled the electric supply of the entire country. We were happy that we enjoyed a good electric power supply during our visit.

During the second week we worked with the Armenian Apostolic Church, as arranged by the Agape staff. Two members of the team worked with nine staff. Two members of the team worked with different groups of laypersons training to be Sunday School teachers. Besides discussing the methods of Christian education with children, they did relational Bible study with the groups. The average size of the groups was about sixty. Both team members gave very enthusiastic reports about the responses of the groups.

The other four traveled by road for six hours over very mountainous regions to work in Lachin where Agape had established a children's home and a building to house volunteers and to conduct community activities. The Director of Agape expressed her appreciation of our work there as follows: "We would like to express our best regards and gratitude to all of you. You did a great job here in Yerevan, Gyumri, many other regions of Armenia and especially in Lachin, as now the Agape Center there serves its main purpose—Christian Education of Children and Youth through the methods you have been demonstrating for a week. It was an excellent start for the center."

Lachin is a link city between Armenia and Karabakh. The ravages of war were everywhere, with more war damaged buildings standing than undamaged ones. Karabakh is a disputed territory that led to the war between Armenia and Azerbaijan. Though there is now a cease fire, the future of the area is in the process of negotiation.

I remember the intensity of everything the children did. Their responses were overwhelming. They hesitantly told of their sufferings when asked. They put up a valiant demonstration of a normal life in extremely difficult circumstances.

Space does not permit me to tell of sightseeing at the Genocide Memorial, the pagan fire temple over which the great ancient Armenian Church is built, the pit where Gregory was imprisoned in 278 A.D. and the story of his miraculous deliverance which led to the conversion of the King and the establishment of the first Christian nation in 301. We also had many wonderful views of Mt. Ararat and recalled the Biblical passages about that mountain and the land of Ararat. We were truly blessed in our sojourn in that historic land with people who still suffer for their faith.

Frances Major
Missionary India-1946-1986
(The Methodist Church, United Methodist Church)
(Submitted 1998)

English Cathedrals from the Choir Loft

 On June 22 twenty-four members of the two adult choirs at Central United Methodist Church [Asheville], including Brooks-Howell residents Roberta Rice and Loise George, piled our "limited" baggage into two vans and drove to the airport at Charlotte, North Carolina. We left from there on British Airways for a flight to Gatwick, London airport, and then on directly to Edinburgh.

There we were met by David Searles, the president of British/European Specialty Tours (BEST). David had sung with the choir of the Canterbury Cathedral for two years and has brought together choirs from all over the USA to sing in festivals in England. There were one hundred eighty one of us who had the magnificent joy and inspiration of singing under the fine direction of David Flood, the organist and choir master at St. Giles Cathedral in Edinburgh. After several hours of rehearsals in the ancient Greyfriar's Kirk we transferred to the St. Giles Cathedral for our first festival concert. This was the church home for John Knox.

Our second stop was at the Yorkminster Cathedral in York, where we had a first-hand view of the beautiful evensong choir. Our Central Church choir then went to the boyhood home of John Wesley in Epworth and sang at the Methodist Church there. A very warm welcome added to the joy of this opportunity.

The second festival concert was at the Canterbury Cathedral, the mother church of all Anglicans. In spite of the fact that they were very busy preparing for the Lambuth Conference, which brings all the Anglican bishops to Canterbury once in ten years, we had the deep joy and inspiration of singing in this world center where so many years ago Thomas a Becket was murdered. Here there is a special shrine to his memory.

The climax of the festival came when we sang at the Westminster Central Hall, the huge Methodist headquarters building across from the British Parliament buildings. Besides the pipe organ, we were accompanied by a special orchestra.

It was a tremendous joy to be on this festival tour. We rested, before the main choir trip home, with a weekend in lovely, picturesque Chipping Camden in the Cotswold.

After the choir left on July 5 for the return trip, I was able to join a cousin who lives in Hertsfordshire, Bushey Heath. We had four exciting days in County Cork, Eire visiting family and old friends. On the return trip to Heathrow lightning hit our plane. The pilot said, "No damage!" We were very thankful!

42

It was good to return to Charlotte, NC on July 21 and a special delight to see Jo Lovelace and Helen Carter, who met us there, after this lifetime, especially inspiring and happy experience of being in the choir lofts of these ancient cathedrals in Great Britain.

Roberta G. Rice, M.D.
Missionary Korea (V.A. Hospital, Grand Island, Nebraska because of the war in Korea 1950-56)
1956-1975
(The Methodist Church, United Methodist Church)
(Submitted 1998)

A Wonderful Trip to Korea

On October 12 I left to go to Korea for the dedication of the new Inchon Community Center building. It was a great surprise to me to be able to go for this special event as one of the guests. I was fortunate to be able to take the place of Maude Groff, who was no longer there. Barbara Pak was with us, and the Rev. Si Rae, the Board representative.

Our tour began with a stop at a coffee house which is operated by handicapped young people. It was a lovely place. They served in such a fine way, and the coffee was good. This project was the dream of the director of the Center, Hyo Soon Han.

The dedication was such an exciting event. Those who had helped to bring about the new building were honored. I was thrilled as I saw several former staff members with whom I had once worked.

The Inchon Center had moved to a new area which allows them to reach out in new programs. They have after school programs, feeding of the elderly, and tutoring classes for students. The facilities are wonderful–they are colorful and will continue to grow.

We did visit the old center and passed a long line of elders who were waiting for their lunch. One surprise was to visit the house where the missionaries once lived. I loved it. It is a two-story building on a hill. The surprise is that the government has taken it over as a landmark, not because we lived there, but because of the architecture. I think that is a compliment to the United Methodist Women.

We were able to visit four other community centers: Pusan,Taejon, Kongju and Tai Wha. Each center has excellent programs, serving the elderly, working with those with disabling conditions (all ages). Taejon and Tai Wha have the only therapeutic pools in the country. We saw a child in the pool receiving therapy, a joy to watch.

There were many other impressions in all the Centers: Korean women learning to read and write Korean, since they had not had the opportunity to go to school; elderly women and children (3 & 4 years old) doing exercises, not easy ones, either. The children were so cute, dressed alike and having the best time. I was amazed at both groups doing such exercises.

We visited the Inchon Hospital, learned about the fine medical staff of two hundred forty-five, with twenty-three medical specialists and nineteen general doctors. As are all hospitals, they are busy and trying to serve the community.

The Methodist Women (under different names) have sent many missionaries, and they planted seeds of service, taking care of people in many areas. It was a thrill to see how the "seeds" have grown in such great ways. This is due to the work of our missionaries, of which we can be proud.

Lucy Gist
Commissioned Deaconess 1950
Executive Director of Community Centers
General Board of Global Ministries,
National Division, Field Representative 1984-1987
Mission Interpreter in Residence,
North Eastern Jurisdiction 1987-1989
Consultant Advance Office (part-time) 1989-2003
(The Methodist Church, United Methodist Church)
(Submitted 2005)

Thirty Years of Growth

It is tomorrow in Korea. Their time is thirteen hours ahead of our summer eastern time. So on Monday, May 2, [2005] I left New York with two friends, going to the 50th reunion of (wartime) medical school graduates from Severance Union Medical School in Seoul, Korea. On Tuesday evening we arrived in the new Incheon International Airport, built by joining islands off the coast of Incheon. We boarded one of the clean, convenient, comfortable buses which travel on the eight-lane new highway and brought us to the new Lotte Hotel near the Duck Soo Palace in downtown Seoul, just a few blocks from our Methodist Mission offices. There in the "like a palace" lobby welcoming me were my angel "social secretary," Mrs. Soon-Hee Lee-Hong, and Dr. Kyung-Sik Kim, a hepatic surgeon from the Yonsei University Medical College. As is the custom, he was to make sure all went well during my visit. At our registration on the 27th floor in the "club area," Dr. and Mrs. Yoon-Soon Kim (he had worked with my brother in postgraduate study in Omaha, NE) were waiting to welcome me. In the post-modern hotel room a beautiful basket of flowers from Dr. Seung ook Sohn, chairman of the department of surgery at Yonsei University (YUMC), added to the welcome. We were welcomed again and again. The next morning our group of overseas guests, invited to the dedication of the new twenty-one stories, 1004 patient bed Severance Hospital, were taken to the Yanghwajin, the Foreigner's Cemetery. The name is derived from the Hans River ferry landing at an historic military site where massive Catholic executions took place in 1839 and 1866. There hundreds of foreigners, many of them good friends with whom I lived and worked, were buried. The Special City of Seoul now protects this lovely site where it is building a large rock and flower garden.

In the afternoon we attended the dedication services for the new Severance Hospital. The ceremony was held at the front of the base of the huge hospital where more than a thousand guests thronged together on a beautiful cloudless afternoon. Hospital patients peered down through the windows. Along the area borders were multiple huge (six feet high) flower frames with congratulation ribbons. Addresses were given by several dignitaries. Perhaps the most listened to was given in Korean by General Leon J. LaPorte of the U.S. Eighth Army. The original Severance Hospital at Yonsei University was built after the Korean War with the help of the U.S. Eighth Army as a memorial to the U.S. soldiers who gave their lives for Korea.

My invitation came from Dr. Hoon-Sang Chi, Vice President for Medical Affairs of Yonsei University, whom I'd known as a surgical resident. He had invited grandchildren of the Avison and Severance families along with those of the architect of the original Severance

45

Hospital built near the south gate of the city in the early 1900's. It was a wonderful example of a culture which remembers and honors its past.

That evening at a delicious dinner at the Grand Hilton we were shown the plans for future development. In an area which has no more land available, long-term plans involve the removal of outdated three-four story buildings with their replacement by high rise contemporary structures built to meet future needs.

Subsequently it was possible to meet many dear and very precious friends, many of whom like me are retired to other opportunities. Everywhere I saw beauty. Every inch of available soil is used for food production and flower growing. The countryside is lined with long plastic greenhouses so that a much greater variety of diet is now available.

It was a special thrill to ride the KTX, the 100 miles per hour new train for the forty-nine minute trip to Deajeon (we called it Taejon) which used to take many hours. Delightful joy included meeting President In-Ryung Shin of Ewha Women's University and Dr. Bock-Hi Woo, a former medical student, who became Vice President of the Ewha Medical Center and is now chairman of the Ewha University Board.

My escorts, Dr. John and Susie Hong of New York, had been the first heads of the Obstetrics & Gynecology, and Pediatric department of our Wonju Union Christian Hospital, which is now the Yonsei University Wonju Medical College and Hospital. Having been at the original hospital ground breaking in the early sixties, it was a happy experience for me to see the tremendous development of that institution along with its contemporary area emergency medical services and excellent communications.

A very delightful day was spent with Mrs. Young Nai Kim-Kang, the widow of Dr. S. B. Kang. He developed the Incheon Christian Hospital and the Ann San University for the training of health science workers. The Lord has done great work through His servants there, many are helped by their Christian witness, and we are very thankful. The whole experience was one of many blessings, joys, delights and happiness, and I give daily thanks to our Lord for His gift of a wonderful lifetime experience along with thanks for all the many persons who helped make it possible. I saw some of the many miracles accomplished by dedicated Christian servants and again and again say, "Praise our Lord and Hallelujah, Hallelujah, Hallelujah!"

Roberta G. Rice, M.D.
Missionary Korea 1956-1976
(V.A .Hospital, Grand Island, Nebraska
because of the war in Korea 1950-56)
(The Methodist Church, United Methodist Church
(Submitted 2005)

46

Jam Cake

Christmas was a great time for our family, Papa, Mama and seven children. About two weeks before, my Mama would make a jam cake, my favorite.

One Christmas she made a most beautiful six-layer job. My mouth was watering with anticipation as she gave us each a thin slice. Mine was too thin, just enough to make me dream of that wonderful day when I could eat all I wanted.

On Monday, everyone went out, including Mama–except that the cake and I were there. I said to myself, "I'm going to get me a real slice of that cake, not too big, but not too little."

I went into Papa and Mama's bedroom, reached into the top drawer of the chest of drawers, and pulled it out. It just kept coming. It came out completely, all over me and all the way to the floor. It did not have the jam cake. It had the eggs for the angel food cake! What a mess!

About that time I heard Mama's footsteps. I knew I was in trouble! She was very serious as she motioned me to sit at the kitchen table. I wondered why. She walked into the bedroom and came back with the cake. She placed it right in front of me, but I was not the least bit hungry. She brought out two plates, one for me and one for her. On mine she placed a great big slice of the cake, and on hers a daintier one. I just sat there. What now? She started eating and motioned for me to do the same. A few moments later she looked up at me with the most beautiful smile I had ever seen and said, "Isn't it good, Ducky?"

What a mother! What a God to make mothers like my Mama!

William (Will) Rogers, Jr.
Missionary Brazil 1939-1963
(The Methodist Church)
(Submitted 2006)

I Remember ...

A Birthday in China

The year was 1927. Chiang Kai Shek's army was marching north from Canton, trying to unify the country. He marched with one division toward Shanghai. Another division which had a Russian advisor and was reported to be anti-American was marching toward Nanking, where I was a language school student. Our American Consulate had warned all "nonessential" Americans in the city to be ready to leave on a moment's notice, if the Consul deemed it necessary.

To this end each of us had packed a "flee" bag with some nonperishable food and a thermos bottle to be filled with boiled water whenever evacuation orders arrived. Since there were no telephones in this city of a million people, the Consul had appointed a contact person in several different areas who would receive emergency messages.

As the invading army neared Nanking, contact persons were notified by Consulate messengers riding bicycles, and our area man reached us. We grabbed our "flee" bags, hopped into a rickshaw, and rushed to the Consulate, which was near the city wall and the Yangtze River. We climbed the city wall from the inside and jumped down on the outside upon a narrow strip of land that bordered the river. Sailors from an American gunboat that was anchored in the middle of the river put us in small boats and quickly headed away from shore. Before we reached safety in the middle of the mile-wide Yangtze River, shots were fired at us by soldiers who had reached the city. When darkness arrived we were removed from the gunboat and taken up river to a British freighter that had unloaded its cargo but could not reload. We climbed up a rope ladder to the ship's deck and then climbed down another ladder to the empty cargo hold. As we stretched out on gunny sacks to sleep, my neighbor looked at her watch and realized it was after midnight. A new day had arrived, my birthday. So she sang "Happy Birthday," to me--on this, my most memorable birthday!

Katherine Ward
Missionary China, Singapore 1925-1939 (Methodist Episcopal Church)
(Married Bishop Ward 1948)
China 1948-1950, Hong Kong & Taiwan 1952-1958
Katherine in Taiwan 1960-1964, Hong Kong 1964-1966
(The Methodist Church)
(Submitted 1996)

A Layman's Sunday

It was laymen's Sunday at the church, and the men of the congregation were doing the various parts of the service. Unfortunately, the man who was to read the Scripture had forgotten to look it up ahead of time. When he reached the platform, he couldn't find the reference, which was in Philippians. He looked in the New Testament and he looked in the Old Testament, repeatedly. Finally, the minister took pity on him and went up and found it for him. The man started to read, and the passage began: "Finally, brethren . . ."

(This occurred in Puerto Rico at the English-speaking white church we attended when I was working there.)

Elizabeth Sterling
Home Missionary 1944-1951
Deaconess USA 1951-1976
(The Methodist Church, United Methodist Church)
(Submitted 1996)

Return to India

After a long journey from Asheville, I arrived in Calcutta, India on May 1, 1996 at 7;00 p.m. I was very tired. My hostess led me to the apartment in the Calcutta Girls' High School where I had lived for many years. Being in familiar surroundings, I relaxed, went to bed early, and slept soundly. The next morning as the day was dawning at about 5:00 a.m., I was awakaned by familiar sounds - the squawking of the crows outside my window and the rattling of  the old trams on the street. Often I had heard my visitors complain about the noise of Calcutta that interrupted their sleep so early in the morning. But to me, on this my first morning back in Calcutta, I was surprised at my own reaction. Those old trams, more than fifty years old, were very noisy. Still running on tracks, they represented an outmoded form of transport. Then why was I enjoying the clattering sound they made?

Then I remembered. Fifty years earlier, when I first arrived in Calcutta, it was a city plagued with communal strife. There were often riots between the Hindus and Muslim people. In 1946, before independence, the two religious groups were equally divided in that city. The Muslims were demanding that Great Britain establish a new nation for the Muslims. Fighting in Calcutta was sometimes fierce. When there was an outbreak of violence, curfew was declared. No one was allowed on the streets. Traffic came to a standstill and the streets were deathly quiet. Unconsciously, I learned to dread the quietness.

When I was awakened by the rattling and clattering of the trams at 5::00 A.M., I knew that there was no curfew and that we could go about our normal activities. So now, fifty years later, on hearing those trams, subconsciously I felt peace. I was at home. I was in a place where I had experienced many things - a place where God had always sustained me. It was a special feeling of awe, wonder and inspiration.

Frances Major
Missionary India 1946-1986;
After retirement, 1987-1989
(The Methodist Church, United Methodist Church)
(Submitted 1996)

When the Phone Rings

Some time ago when I walked into the front lobby the phone rang and the call was for me. The young woman calling identified herself as the daughter of my friend who was the secretary of Fair Haven United Methodist Church, where I was on the staff as Director of Christian Education. Yes, I remembered her parents, sister and brother. She was born later. She and her husband came to see me. They took pictures of my TEXAS PICTURE painted by her mother thirty-five years ago!

I recall many experiences of this young church on the edge of Houston. We had three sessions of Sunday School, two morning worship services in our large fellowship hall, Nursery, Kindergarten (also weekday) and Elementary classrooms. Then there were my office and supply room at the end, before turning to the Youth Center. In the parking lot we had a Boy Scout cabin.

I remember:

--Melissa, age four, who came with her mother, Youth Superintendent. One day when they were driving past the church with her older sisters, Melissa said, "There is where God and Miss Hoffman live." I appreciated that!

--Bob, a third grader, told his mother about a new family with a boy his age, and he said "Mother, can't we <u>invite</u> them to our Church?" They came!

--At Christmas we built an outdoor Nativity scene with a live cow and calf, lambs, and a donkey. A young couple asked to be married in front of this lighted scene. As the minister pronounced them husband and wife, the donkey let out a big "heehaw, heehaw." Yes, they had their pictures taken together.

I remember many interesting people and events. Now, my special TEXAS PICTURE is more special since I have met another of LaMerle's family.

Sara Gene Hoffman
Deaconess USA
1937-1977
(Methodist Episcopal Church,
The Methodist Church, United Methodist Church)
(Submitted 1997)

Accidentally in Fidel's Caravan

Fulgencio Batista and his entourage left Cuba the night of December 31, 1958, so Fidel and his bearded rebels woke up January 1, 1959 to discover they had won the revolution. They were up in the mountains in easternmost Oriente province, so they began their trek, going through all the provinces, Camaguey, LasVillas, Matanzes, la Habana, Pinar del Rio.

I arrived in Cuba in August 1957 to teach at the Methodist Colegio Irene Toland in Matanzas. At the Annual Conference in 1958 another Methodist missionary, Joyce Hill (no relation) was appointed to the rural center Santa Rosa in sugar cane country in Matanzas province. In December of that year the District Superintendent felt that it was too dangerous for Joyce to be out there alone, so he told her to come into Matanzas to stay at the school. Later in January Joyce began to worry because she had left food in the gas refrigerator, and she was afraid that the gas had run out; so she invited me to go with her to Santa Rosa to see. Yes, the gas had run out, so you can imagine what the kitchen smelled like with the food spoiling in the refrigerator! We set to work cleaning it out, but all the time Joyce had an ear listening to her transistor radio to find out where Fidel was. When she heard that he was approaching Jovellanos, the nearest town, we jumped into the jeep to go see him as he passed. We saw him and his motley crew of bearded rebels. We were then ready to go back to Mantanzas, but there was no way we could get ahead of him or pass him up, so we had to fall in behind. He went slowly, and often made stops to greet the people in every settlement along the way, so it took us forever to arrive in Matanzas. It was already dark when we got here. Fidel was to appear in the plaza that night, but we had seen enough. Being in a jeep, we were greeted along the way as though we were one of his caravan. The people had high hopes for what Fidel could do for the country, but many were soon disappointed. At this time Fidel said he was a "humanist" and waited more than two years to confess that he was a Marxist-Leninist Communist.

Helen L. Hill
Missionary 1948-1960—Study and Cuba
1961-1993—Mexico, working with Cuban refugees
(The Methodist Church, United Methodist Church)
(Submitted 1997)

Life at Red Bird Mission

The eight hundred fifty miles between Iowa and Kentucky were behind us and our family of four were settled in a store building at Mill Creek waiting for a stone parsonage to be built Although there were no modern facilities there in 1946, we did have running water. When it rained rivulets ran over the kitchen shelves and Arthur drilled holes in the wooden floor for run off!

I was attempting to iron with sadirons warmed on a step-stove, when three new little friends came by. Margaret, the oldest, asked, "Are there some big Sunday School pictures we can take to Creasy and Turner? They are both sick and we want to visit them up Powderhorn."

I was glad to leave the iron on the stove and go about twenty rods to the church house with these delightful girls in charming feedsack dresses. They laid down their wild flowers on a pew and selected Bible scenes which would brighten any log cabin.

I wish I could have responded to the customary invitation, "Go with us," but I demurred and returned to my ironing. They surprised me a few hours later by stopping at the church house where I happened to be.

"Oh, we had the best time. Creasy and Turner cried and we sang and prayed and gave them the pictures," Margaret said.

How blessed I was to know children like these and help them on their spiritual journey! Before Margaret left, she summed it all up with, "Oh, I just love to make people happy."

These girls and ten others, along with my own son and daughter (later another daughter was born at Red Bird Mission Hospital), and a few boys from time to time were my life for eight years at the little white church house on Mill Creek.

Postscript: Turner and Creasy were a loveable couple who came to the Post Office from time to time. She was usually ahead and he followed on the narrow path. Arthur took a picture of them and later called them to the house to see the revealing and large projected slide.

They looked for a long time in amazement, and Creasy broke the silence with, "Law me, Turner, if'n I'd know'd you was that much taller than me, I'd a dug a hole and put you down in it."

Esther Russell
Home Missionary Red Bird Mission, Kentucky
1946-1966
(Evangelical United Brethren, United Methodist Church)
(Submitted 1997)

My Arrival in Japan

It was a hot muggy day, September 5, 1956, when I first stepped foot on the shores of   Japan.   To tell the truth, my first impression was disappointing. One word would describe it -- drab. I guess I had expected the green of a quiet Oriental temple garden. The country still had not recovered from the ravages of the war. This was evident not only during the trip by car from the port in Yokohama but also on the campus of Aoyama Gakuin in Tokyo where I was to serve as a short-term missionary for the next three years. That afternoon we traveled over what was called "the main highway." It was a cacophonous mass of bicycles, motor scooters, motor cycles, three-wheelers, buses and autos. Down the middle of the narrow thoroughfare ran double streetcar tracks. The rough winding highway was lined with row after row of small shops open to the street, revealing a cluttered confusion of merchandise. From second floor windows above the shops hung the laundry and bedding of the shopkeepers' families. That, of course, was over forty years ago. Aoyama Gakuin itself was still in the process of rebuilding and there was no central heating that first winter. Sometimes my fingers were so stiff from the cold that I could not write on the blackboard.

I arrived at the beginning of what is in the Japanese school year the second semester, so all my classes were hand-me-downs. From the new school year in April 1957 I had "my own" classes, most of them freshmen oral English in the economics department. I also

54

taught one section of advanced English composition to juniors in the English literature department. It took a lot of time, but I enjoyed it immensely. The English lit majors were more mature and had a better command of English than did the freshmen Econ majors. As a result of my experience those first years in Japan I became convinced of the important role that Christian schools have to play in the evangelization of Japan. That conviction grew stronger through the years as I observed the life pilgrimages of some of my early students.

One good example was Ken Yamada, a student in that first composition class. In one of his compositions he wrote the following:

Our school, Aoyama Gakuin . . . has been noted for its 'Christian spirit' since its beginning. It is quite true that every student who enters this school has doubts about what kind of religion Christianity is. Here every student can find clear and complete answers to these doubts. We study Christianity itself and the Bible. . . . We are aided further to understand by attending the worship service in the chapel every day. . . . I have studied in this university for the past two years. . . . I have not visited the campus of any other university without feeling something completely different. At first I could not understand why I felt this way. I learned the reason as days went by. It is the Christian atmosphere here. This is what made me feel all the more keenly the joy of being a student of Aoyama Gakuin University.

Ken was baptized soon after this, and after a few years came to the States, where he earned a doctor's degree and eventually came under the employment of our UMC General Board of Higher Education and Ministry. There as Associate General Secretary he has made a unique and significant contribution to strengthening international ties among Methodist colleges and schools around the world and to the founding and development of Africa University. His life pilgrimage has led him to an opportunity for service which neither he nor I could have imagined in those days forty years ago in cold, gray drab postwar Japan.

John W. Krummell
Missionary Japan 1956-1959, 1961-1996
(The Methodist Church, United Methodist Church

Submitted 1997

Caught in a Fire at Payne College

Because Paine College needed all its room for the faculty members, I had moved to the home of a young family. The father was away on business. I had made it clear to the mother that I would be glad to help if ever she needed me.

Consequently, one evening after I came home from school, I found the mother with her baby at the door, concern in her face. She asked if I would go down to the cellar to check on the furnace for her. Of course,I went immediately, only to be confronted by an explosion! As I stood there, suddenly Richard Stenhouse, head of the Philosophy and Religion Department at Paine, arrived. It seemed that somehow he knew there was trouble. He came straight over to me. Immediately, somehow he found wood to make a resting place for me, and then called the nearby hospital for help. He worked with water he found nearby to help my burning flesh.

The hospital staff responded quickly. They packed me in their van, with Richard going along. It was a splendid job they did with me, so that in an amazingly short time I could be released. Richard had the double load of teaching for some time at Paine College. He did so well that students went right on with their work in our division of philosophy and religion, as well, if not better, than usual.

Never, I believe, could we forget the amazing gift of Richard Stenhouse. He gave as he picked up both the faculty loads of teaching and as he continued to visit me at the hospital until I had recovered enough to get back to Paine College and to teach.

I cannot tell you the year or the time of the year, except that the weather out-of-doors seemed to offer no problem. How I regret that I kept no personal records.

Cecelia Sheppard

Taught at Lucy Webb Training School (for deaconesses) for 2 years; the Kansas City Training School; the Fellowship of Reconciliation; with the American Friends Service Committee in Mexico for three months; Penn College in Okaloosa, Iowa; in an experimental Work and Study Community under Earlham College; and finally in Paine College where she taught for twenty-two years (a United Methodist related historically black college).

(Submitted 1997)

Down Memory Lane with MIRIAM JEAN GRUBER

I REMEMBER - Mid-August of 1948 when I first arrived in China. Our commuter plane from Shanghai landed at Foochow's little air strip cut out of the middle of a rice paddy. No one was there to meet me except a few rice farmers with whom communication was possible only through smiles! Their Foochow dialect and my one year of Mandarin language study at Yale did not provide adequately for conversation. However, after about thirty minutes, Dr. Lucy Wang, president of Hwa Nan College, Dr. Ivy Chou, my dear friend and principal of Hwa Nan High School, arrived with the senior missionary, the Rev. Henry Lacy. They were profuse in their apologies for the unavoidable delay in meeting me.

I REMEMBER - One very happy year of making friends, learning to love China, enjoying Chinese food, and teaching at Hwa Nan where I also helped with the chapel services. These activities and further language study occupied my time.

I REMEMBER - August of 1949 when the Red Army took over Foochow. The curtailment of our Christian work began.

I REMEMBER - April of 1950 when our Hwa Nan High School principal faced public trial as she was accused of being too "Westernized" because she had spent two years as a Crusade Scholar while studying at Scarritt College, Columbia University and Union Seminary in the USA.

I REMEMBER - June of 1950 when a precious Chinese Christian was executed after having been accused of being "a running dog of the Americans."

I REMEMBER - November of 1950 when the last of us foreign missionaries in Foochow, except Bishop Lacy, were granted exit permits, and the long, prescribed circuitous journey from Foochow via Canton to Hong Kong and FREEDOM began. (Bishop Lacy later died in Foochow.)

I REMEMBER - Late December of 1950 when I left my America-bound co-workers on board the B. & O. liner to continue their journey to the USA. I remained in Singapore because I had accepted the invitation from the resident Bishop, Raymond Archer, to stay and help with the work in the Methodist schools and churches.

I had the privilege of spending the next two and one-half decades at assignments by the Bishop to work in Singapore and Malaysia. In Singapore, besides assisting at the

Methodist schools and churches I was the Chaplain of the Girls' Brigade and overseer of the Methodist Guest House. In Malaysia I was "mama" to one hundred twenty girls who lived at our hostel while attending school. A Local Pastor's License offered me opportunity to expand my work beyond the home.

I REMEMBER -- A great many events occurring around the world and in my own life during the years between1950-1979. Particularly, I recall:

August 9, 1965 when the 150-year Crown Colony of Singapore became the REPUBLIC OF SINGAPORE (a City State), at which time it was the 116th nation to join the United nations.

September of 1979 when I was officially retired by the Board of Global Ministries under the Women's Division.

October of 1979 when I received a non-censored letter from a former co-worker in Foochow that the first openly-approved worship service was held in our Church of Heavenly Peace in that city.

And I REMEMBER my retirement years with great joy over its many avenues of continued volunteer missionary service in Singapore and Malaysia in the 80's, and my time at Brooks-Howell home from 1995 to the present.

Miriam Gruber
Missionary China 1946-1950,
Singapore 1950-1953, 1963-1969
Malaysia 1954-1963,
Southeast Asia Office of Board 1975
(The Methodist Church, United Methodist Church)
(Submitted 1997)

Just a Day's Work

 I stepped out of a little church where I had been speaking to the Woman's Missionary Society and looked at my watch. Ten p.m.—I should be home in an hour. I turned into the New York Thruway and made my way into the middle lane to make better time. Suddenly, I heard a noise under the car. Oh, no! That muffler loose again? By now the fast-moving milk trucks were on either side of me, but I had to slow down.

A big milk truck drew up on my right side and the driver was about to yell at me for going slow in that lane. I pointed down, and he understood.. He slowed down and signaled the truck on my left. He slowed down too, and motioned that I should turn off at the next exit, which was about two miles down the road. As we approached the turn, he slowed down and let me pass in front of him. This I did with fear and trembling. To my surprise, he followed me out. When I stopped at a gas station, he stopped and came to my window. "What is a little gal like you doing out running around the Thruway this hour of night?" he asked.

Then he saw my deaconess dress. "Are you a Sister, or something?"

"Yes," I said "a Sister—or something!"

He walked away, saying, "It figures!"

I pulled into our parking lot at midnight. Sister Linda was at the door. "I've been so worried—are you all right"

I answered, "All right . See you in the morning."

If you want some excitement in your life—ride the New York Thruway along with the milk trucks, at midnight!

Nina Leedham
Deaconess USA 1926-1929;
Married, re-consecrated as a deaconess in 1955-1974
Volunteered for 10 years after retirement
(Methodist Episcopal Church,
The Methodist Church, United Methodist Church)
(Submitted 1998)

The Night I Danced in the *Carnaval*

Yes, I remember the night I danced in the *Carnaval*. It was one of my experiences while serving through the Central Methodist Church in Salvador in the state of Bahia, Brazil. There the city goes all-out to celebrate popular festivals all summer long, which, in that part of the world, lasts from the end of December through March or longer. *Carnival* is the major celebration. It is a magic spectacle with all-out celebration—the poor, the rich, black, white, mulatto. That means practically everybody except the members of the Protestant churches, who often have retreats out away from the centers.

The Bahia region is where the majority of the slaves from Africa were brought to do the manual labor in the cotton and sugar cane fields. So the African influence of their gods, customs and food is felt strongly there.

I went every Sunday by bus to a poor section of the city, called "Liberdade," where our church had a new congregation, for Sunday School in the morning, visitation in the afternoon and a worship service in the evening.

So, after the worship service of that *Carnaval* Sunday evening, I took the bus back to the center, the end of the line. My apartment, however, was on the other side of the main street. That made it necessary for me to cross the main stream of the *Carnaval* celebration. The huge truck bearing electric instruments playing *samba* music was passing by, and the street was filled to overflowing with people, dressed in all sorts of costumes. Some were in groups, dressed alike. Others were just joining in with the rhythm, dancing to the music, others just "jumping" along.

I waited a while. What to do? Finally, because there seemed no other option, I plunged in, "jumping" too. I was carried along for some distance before reaching the other side and continued to my nearby apartment. From there I could still hear the jubilant sounds until early morning. That is a *Carnival* I will never forget, since I, too, danced in the *Caraival*!

Frances Burns
Wesley Foundation, Director,
East Texas University in Commerce—1945-1949
Missionary Brazil 1949-1979
(The Methodist Church, United Methodist Church)
(Submitted 1998)

An Adventure in Travel

June 14, 1971 started as an adventure when four middle-aged American women left West Berlin in a four-door Opel with Swiss license plates, headed west, then north to Hamburg. What we failed to realize was that the Autobahn was the only legal route that would take us to Copenhagen via Hamburg. We opted for a shorter route going northwest, leaving the Autobahn. We found ourselves in East Germany's narrower, rougher roads, some under construction, which slowed our progress considerably. The atmosphere seemed austere and unfriendly. Waiting for a train to cross a one-lane railroad bridge further detained us. We next encountered a convoy of East German troops on manoeuvre. A military officer stopped us, but since we did not speak German we were unable to respond. Pointing to the word "lost" in the English-German dictionary got us off the hook. At the last checkpoint before going into West Germany the guard took our passports to the guardhouse. He returned to the car with an interpreter asking such questions as "What are you doing here?" "Where have you been since the last checkpoint?" They consulted with each other and delivered the bad news. We must turn back, retrace our steps and pick up the Autobahn where we turned off at least one hundred fifty miles back. The four of us looked at the interpreter in disbelief. We were to turn back immediately, not stopping for food or lodging, and were to be out of East Germany by midnight. It was then 9:00 p.m. One request the guard could not deny. We four badly needed the "toiletten." He let us go in the guardhouse one at a time. Greatly disappointed and fearful, we turned the car around.

By this time it was pitch dark and a fine drizzle settled on the windshield. The street lights were dim. The gas indicator was of great concern. Running out of gas under these circumstances was not funny. Their system of dispensing gas was unknown to us. One found an Intertank by locating a large blue light. A series of lockers containing a litre each of gas could be opened with a key—but who had a key?? By chanced we spotted a young couple walking on the street. "Intertank!" we called out. "Ya," came the reply. One of them spoke English. Glory be! He explained about the key. The young woman had an uncle, a priest, who lived next door. The couple brought two keys with our American dollars. It was close to 2:00 a.m. when the lights of the Autobahn came into view. The guard at the check point pointed to the time stamped on our passport and to his watch and looked at us as if to say, "Where have you been?" Our driver pointed on the map the route we took. A comprehending look spread across his face and he waved us on. The unanimous vote among us was to keep going until we boarded the ferry to Copenhagen. This we did gladly and gratefully!

Lucille Bovet
Educator (Special Education);
Lived with Deaconess May Titus for many years
(The Methodist Church, United Methodist Church)
(Submitted 1998)

Surgery in Korea During a Revolution

One of the more memorable times of my service as a surgeon and medical educator in Korea came on April 19, I believe it was in 1963, the time of the student revolution when the "Grandpa President," Syngman Rhee, was overthrown after his fourth election as the president of the Republic of Korea.

The morning of April 19 I operated at our Ewha Woman's University Medical Hospital at the East Gate of Seoul. A patient needing a colon resection for cancer was scheduled in the afternoon at Severance Hospital, the Yonsei Medical Hospital located near the South Gate of Seoul.

As we left the East Gate area and drove by Seoul National University Hospital area the streets were filling with students. I particularly remember the medical students from SNU in their white coats. They were marching, carrying signs, and protesting the fraudulent recent election by shouting and singing.

The colon resection operation at Severance proceeded smoothly but, as we were completing it, we could hear the sounds of gunfire outside the hospital. Also, we suddenly saw a growing pillar of black smoke out of the north window. The students had set the government newspaper offices on fire because of its failure to tell truly what was going on. The police were shooting the students demonstrating on the streets outside the hospital.

In a short time we had more than one hundred students with gunshot wounds fill the downstairs halls. We operated throughout the night and until late the next afternoon. First came those with chest wounds, then the abdominal wounds; the orthopedic patients came after we general surgeons were finished. Supplies ran short. Sponges were rewashed and sterilized. Students poured in to give blood. We lost our first patient. He had been hit by a "dumdum" which exploded, damaging and destroying his bladder and lower abdomen.

The nineteenth day of April will always be a sad remembrance day in Korea. About one hundred students were killed by police bullets on that day.

My cancer patient disappeared that night. After he left the operating room he was hidden in a closet. He had been head of the government ministry which was responsible for much of the corruption that led to the revolution. Eventually he ended in prison. We were able to keep a good follow-up on him for several years. As far as I know he had a complete recovery.

Many prayers were prayed at that time. Several of the dead students had been Christians. The nation mourned their deaths with a national monument at their graves. Korea will always remember the nineteenth of April and the way in which students died for their beliefs in freedom and democracy.

Roberta G. Rice, M.D.
Missionary Korea 1956-1976
(The Methodist Church, United Methodist Church)

(Submitted 1998)

"I'm Going to Make It!"

 Marissa walked into the "free world" after eighteen months behind the walls of a state prison, carrying a small bag of belongings and a big smile. The first two persons to greet her were United Methodist Women. Representatives from several United Methodist Churches provided her basic needs during those first crucial days.

Marissa enrolled in Nashville Technical Institute and found a job, where she received encouragement and praise for her work.

A year later emergency surgery, followed by a stroke, left her partially paralyzed. Six months of therapy resulted in her learning to walk again—with the help of a cane. She learned to write and to talk more distinctly.

She had declared from the beginning, "I'm going to make it! I know I will."

To become more independent and take responsibility for her two children, Marissa reentered the technical school to prepare for work as an accountant.

We taxpayers were investing $3,960 per year in government subsidies for Marissa's future. In prison the cost would have teen $10,000, and she would have had little opportunity to prepare herself for becoming a productive citizen.

One Sunday morning Marissa walked slowly with her cane to the front of the sanctuary of Edgehill United Methodist Church to confess her faith and make her vows to the church.

"I feel good. You have accepted me. You are my family, so I have someone to turn to, to be with. I don't feel alone with my problems."

It was not easy for Marissa to learn to trust people, but her ability to trust her life and gifts to the church and community continued to grow.

Marissa maintains stoutly that she is "going to make it!" Sometimes she says it with frustration and through tears, but always she says it with determination and faith—faith in God, her church community, and herself.

Laura B. Wells
Church & Community Worker 1958-1994
Commissioned a Deaconess 1989
(The Methodist Church, United Methodist Church)
(Submitted 1998)

My Year in the Philippines

It was Christmas Eve, 1968, during the fourth month of my year as Exchange Deaconess in the Philippines. My co-worker (Conference Director of Youth Work) and I (Conference Deaconess) started our journey to attend the first of the three district Christmas institutes for youth, held each year between December 26 and December 31. This one was the farthest away, so we went there first, traveling by bus that afternoon to the home where we joined the pastor and a youth we would accompany to the meeting.

After spending the night, we quickly downed a sweet roll and left at 5:00 a.m. on foot to where we could board a *Jeepney* to the bus station. The "baby bus" took us to a place where we joined four other passengers in an old car, in order to get the ferry across a body of water before the bus we had to take left at noon. From the ferry we took a horse-drawn cart to the bus station. It was noon and our bus was already full and ready to leave. We were in need of food—and a "comfort room."

The bus driver took pity on us and waited for us to have a meal at the bus station canteen. We hurriedly ate our Christmas menu of two small cubes of pork fat, some rice and the luxury of a Pepsi which had been refrigerated. In the meantime the driver had made space for us on the very dilapidated-looking vehicle. Bus breakdowns were frequent, but this one had no mechanical problems that day.

We rode as far as the bus went, not many kilometers from the village of our destination on the north shore of Mindanao. Our last ride was behind the drivers of four motorcycles. Lina and I received the usual fine hospitality of a family in their home. Our hostess prepared for us our real Christmas dinner, complete with squid, rice and vegetables. We were more than ready for a good night's rest.

(During my year in the Philippines I spent one or more nights in over one hundred homes, experiencing true Filipino hospitality. What a blessing!)

Anne McKenzie
Deaconess, Rural Worker
(Church & Community Worker) U.S.A. 1948-1988

(One year in the Philippines 1967-1968)
(The Methodist Church, United Methodist Church)

(Submitted 1998)

Life at Allen School in 1959*

 The school year was 1959. With school integration problems tearing local communities apart we at Allen High School found ourselves close by and involved in a nearby community. High school African-American girls from the community long ago had discovered Allen as a boarding school meeting their family needs. At the opening of the 1959 school year matters came to a head and a boycott by the black community meant that alternative schools must be found. With strength from families in the community, guidance from the American Friends Service Committee, and growing support all over the country, we at Allen found that our resources, too, could be used. These included taking in all the high school students, including four teen-age boys, into our all-female school. I particularly remember that they decided to elect as their extra-curricular activity the glee club—about forty girls and four boys. A challenge for the music teacher!

The following year tension subsided, the community moved ahead in good faith, and the four boys, as I remember, joined the student body at Asheville's public white school, and found the school needed them especially on the basketball squad.

*Allen High School was a Woman's Division school for African-American Girls in Asheville, NC.

Winifred Wrisley
Deaconess USA Allen High School 1955-1968,
Harwood School, New Mexico, 1968- 1974;
Special Appointment, Vermont 1975-198 8;
(The Methodist Church, United Methodist Church)
(Submitted 1999)

Transporting a Precious Bundle

The work of the revision of the New Testament in the Hausa language in Northern Nigeria had been "in the making" for some years. With all the many "little" things that must be carefully cared for, and the work checked, checked, and checked again before it could be called "ready for print," time--yes years—passed by.

Finally that wonderful day came when all was ready. Those of us working on it held the manuscript, and together we sang "Praise God from Whom All Blessings Flow." It was truly a wonderful day.

But, we then realized there was one more hurdle. The printing must be done in London by the British and Foreign Bible Society. How do we get this most precious bundle safely to London? Well, it was wrapped—and it seemed such a very, very small package to have taken so many years to produce, to be so important and to contain such precious words. The package was tied to the back of a bicycle, and one of the translators took it to the local post office. There was nothing else to do but trust to the international mail system.

Yes, finally it got to London, and eventually the completed Hausa New Testament was in our hands. Again "Praise God from Whom All Blessings Flow."

Lucy Rowe
Missionary Nigeria 1946-1952, 1957-1963;
Sarawak, Malaysia 1964-1968
(Evangelical United Brethren Church, United Methodist Church)

(Submitted 1999)

Some Recollections of Genesis

(No references whatsoever to the biblical book)

(Tennessee, Early 1940s)

All aboard for the Saturday Night Community Meeting at the one-room elementary school in Genesis! (It was the *only* meeting place of any kind there.) I climbed into the station wagon for the sixteen-mile drive on a gravel road from Crossville. The winding road went over hills, crossed mountain streams and threaded through the beautiful Catoosa Forest and Game Reserve. A few small houses dotted the road along the way.

After I parked the car the young people helped unload supplies and get the room ready for the meeting. The Coleman lanterns were lit and hung on the hooks suspended from the ceiling. The folding organ was set up, and the Cokesbury Worship Hymnals were brought in.

I let the tailgate of the station wagon down to give access to the three-shelf library, the first in the county. Both youth and adults began selecting books and magazines to check out. When this was completed, we went inside to share what had happened in the community during the week.

A hymn sing of favorites followed. Since there were no churches, and they were not holding religious services in the community, they asked that I have devotions to close the activities each week. I agreed to do this, but explained that I was not a preacher.

One evening only four people had come because of the rain. Everybody had to walk, and carry lanterns to light the way. The four who came were all youth. They decided they needed to start home early because of the bad weather. We had sung a closing hymn when we heard voices and saw lantern light through the windows. An entire family of five came in. They had walked a mile and a half to get there.

The Lord very plainly spoke to me, saying, "Give the devotions!" I did, with their consent. During the closing prayer I gave an opportunity for anyone who had not accepted Christ as their Savior to do so in their hearts then. After the prayer we said goodbyes and went home.

The following Saturday night when I came over the last hill, the school building was ablaze with light. There was a crowd, both in the yard and inside. Horses and mules were hitched and a flatbed truck was parked in the yard. I was at a loss to understand what was going on. When I got out of the car a man of small stature came over and asked, "Are you Miss Marthy?"

"Yes," I replied.

"Please come inside," he invited.

We all went inside, and I learned that this man was "Squire" McCoy, the elected official representing that section in the county governing body. He went to the front and said, "My grandson was converted in you meeting last Saturday and we've all come to show our appreciation and thanks."

From that moment on we had won the confidence of the people and made progress in working together to help them improve their quality of life. I reflected on all this and remembered how we had almost dismissed without the devotions and prayer.

I learned two important lessons that night that I have never forgotten: (1) That God works in strange ways to get His work done; and (2) that I was never to judge the success or failure of anything in terms of numbers.

(Originally published in *Along the Way, Stories by Church and Community Workers in Kaleidoscope Ministry,* compiled by The History Committee of the Church and Community Workers Organization, related to the Office of Church and Community Ministry, National Program Division, General Board of Global Ministries, The United Methodist Church, 1986. Used by permission of the chair of the Church and Community Workers Organization History and Archives Committee.)

Martha Almon
Deaconess USA 1938-1945, 1948-1976
(Methodist Episcopal Church, South,
The Methodist Church, United Methodist Church)

(Submitted 1999)

An Alcoholic Who Was Saved

One day, about midmorning, there was an urgent clapping at the front gate. Lavinia was there—along with Martinho, a convert of about ten days. I first met Martinho when Lavinia, one of the founding members of our fledgling church, took him to the worship service.

The services were held in our house, so every Sunday night we would rearrange the furniture, set up chairs and open the folding pump organ. On that particular night, when Lavinia arrived with Martinho and another friend of his, we could hardly breathe! Those two men were not only dirty, but they reeked with the smell of alcohol! They behaved themselves quite well, and at the end of the service when Leon* gave an opportunity to accept Christ, Martinho suddenly stood—"I want to be a Christian!"

After praying with him and answering his questions and warning him that it probably would not be easy to change his way of life, we saw a new glow in his eyes. He declared, "Pastor, I'm not drinking another drop!"

This forty-year-old man had learned to drink *cachaça* at his father's knee at the age of five. Now, here he was in my room—shaking like a leaf!

"I want to talk to the pastor. I've got to talk to him! He's got to pray for me!"

"He isn't here right now."

"Then you must pray for me! I don't want to drink, but I want to. I can't stand it!"

"But the pastor won't be back before noon."

"Then you must pray for me!"

So we prayed. I gave him a supply of hard candies and a supply of vitamins, instructing him, "When you have the urge to drink, pop candy into your mouth and get busy doing something. Ask God to help you. We'll be praying for you too."

I'll never forget the day Martinho and his common law wife exchanged marriage vows. They made their profession of faith, joined the church, received holy communion, and were married—all in the same service!

*Leon was Martha's husband, the pastor.

70

Martha Strunk
Missionary Brazil—Woman's Division
1950-1953,
Board of Missions, World Division
1959-1992
Volunteer in Brazil 1992-1998
(The Methodist Church, United Methodist Church)
(Submitted 1999)

Experiences of a Dorm Parent

It was a challenge to put thirty boys, third grade through seventh, to bed. It was my privilege to do so at Navajo Methodist School, Farmington, New Mexico, when Leland* was in another dorm relieving the dorm parent. Usually, everything went along smoothly. One night, however, the boys had gone up the two flights of stairs to their bedrooms as usual, and I followed. When I came to the first room where five boys should be, not a boy was in sight. I gasped, but before I could say a word I saw Tony's toe sticking out from under his bed. I went around and  had a story and prayer with the other boys. When I was ready to go downstairs, all five boys were in bed. They had done it so quietly that I had not heard them. They mentioned nothing about the trick they planned to play. It was the only time they went to bed under their beds.

We read stories to the boys after they were settled in their beds. One night I finished *Gentle Ben*. The next night when I read a new story, Edison said, "What happened to *Gentle Ben*?" Another time Leland was reading *Ajax*, the story of an Australian wild dog. The boys could be heard saying, "Ajax, Ajax" as they went up the stairs.

My heart really took a tumble when I once went to check the boys and Willie was not in his bed. I rejoiced and gave thanks when I found him in bed with Ron.

*Leland was her husband.

Elizabeth Dellinger
Home Missionary Alaska, 1938-1942;
Farmington, NM 1945-1973
(Submitted 1999)

Christmas in India

My memories of Christmas celebrations in India are so varied. Let me share with you some of them. My first South India Christmas in a girls' boarding school was celebrated one month early—November 25. A month later the girls would be in their homes with their families—about one hundred twenty-five in Christian homes and thirty in Hindu homes. In the open-sided school chapel with its thatched roof over a sandy floor the girls in their white *saris* sat on individual woven mats. Covered heads and bare feet were outward signs of worship and reverence. The  Christmas scriptures and carols set this day apart. The mid-day Christmas feast of special rice and curry with coconut and nuts added to the occasion. The school hall was decorated with streamers of yellow and green twisted crepe paper (yellow is a happy color). A fun program in the evening brought the happy day to a close.

Churches in India are usually full on Christmas Day. It is a day to wear new clothes, to wear freshly picked flowers, to give and receive garlands and sweets, to have open house and to decorate with balloons. After church everyone goes home to a meal with something special. Hindu and Muslim neighbors visit Christian families. Religious differences are forgotten in the atmosphere of joy and celebration.

One Christmas in Lucknow a professor at Isabella Thoburn College joined me in inviting several Christian Africans who were studying at the university to join us for Christmas dinner. Special rice and curry! Yum! Yum! It was a bright sunny day, so we ate on the verandah and looked out at the hedge of six-foot poinsettias in the front garden. There was no need for artificial ornaments.

In the evening I visited a Christian community outside Lucknow where all the musical instruments of the village were brought out, including a large drum. The cacophony of the "band" needed all the space of out-of-doors. The joy and happiness of this group of Christians was expressed in volume if not in harmony!

Christmas for Christians in India is focused, joyous and unsophisticated.

Eunice Sluyter
Missionary
Dates unknown:India for 5 years (Reformed Church)
5 years: Isabella Thoburn College
(United Methodist Church)
5 years: Publisher, Lucknow Publishing House
(United Methodist Church)
(Submitted 1999)

Christmas in Rural Oregon

Snow had fallen during the night, a few inches of Oregon high desert snow that crunched with sound and feel under my boots. There, in the snow, I saw a trail of small footprints. Two or three children had turned onto the road from the path to the artesian well and walked toward Babe's store. The footprints stopped in front of the manger scene in the vacant lot by the store. The lighted plastic figures of Joseph and Mary and the baby, donated by Carol, had withstood the December weather well. Through the Christmas season I had noticed that the snow in front of the manger scene was always scuffed and disturbed by boots of all sizes.

Now, Christmas was over and Epiphany had come, and it was time to think of taking down and storing the figures for another year. Bob and Kenny, who had built the stable and manger, had taken responsibility for dissembling and storing them. The psychedelic star over the stable would be put on the storage shelf at the church. The star had surprised several drivers and almost caused a wreck. One of the church members had suggested that next year we should put a sign at the top of the hill: "Danger! Startling Star ahead!"

This year, Christmas had been a time of inviting the community into the small United Methodist Church in Beatty. Drawing on their memories, the congregation had planned well and issued invitations, both verbal and written, to all. The community had come! As I stood in front of the manger scene on Epiphany, I remembered how on Christmas Eve we had sat and eaten, crowded shoulder to shoulder in the rough-floored social hall, as we reestablished the custom of a shared potluck feast. Harry* had built a strong fire in the huge old wood stove, and pots simmered on it.

After we had eaten, parents and grandparents of the children had been invited to the sanctuary to visit while other adults from the community had helped the children make a gift for their mothers and fathers or grandparents. As the children had finished their gifts, they had made paper chains and strung popcorn to decorate the church. Native and non-Native generations mixing in this rural church had been a natural development, and we hoped had set a pattern.

During the worship service we had sung Christmas carols and heard special numbers sung by our eight-person community choir who were making their first appearance. Proudly, but a bit abashed, they had stood and sung in choir robes loaned by First Church in Klamath Falls. The pastor had brought us a message, brief and simple, and as Luke's story of the incarnation was read, many lips were moving, people whispering the story with him.

The presence of Santa Claus was required because that was part of the tradition. Sleigh bells had jingled, and we had sung, "Here Comes Santa Claus." Here he was, in a red suit with baby powder in his beard and a pack pull of candy for everyone and small gifts for the children.

As we gathered to wish each other "Merry Christmas," the groups that made up our community had hugged, pounded shoulders, and mixed that night. Native people who had grown up on a reservation, only to see it terminated, ranchers and retirees who had bought up land to live the simple life, leftover flower children who perched on the side of the mountain and had come down to celebrate.

We all knew what "Emmanuel" meant that night in Beatty, Oregon. Now, we knew, it was time to go on and live out together an Epiphany that would share God's love with those like us and those unlike us.

*Harry Janzen, Ann's husband.

Ann Perry Janzen
Church and Community Worker USA
1968-1983, 1987-1989
Deaconess—Commissioned 1979

UMCOR 1989 St. Croux (3 months)
1990- 1992 Volunteer in Aleutian Islands, Alaska

(United Methodist)
(Submitted 2000)

Difficult Days in Sierra Leone

It was April 16, 1953, in the third year of my first term in Sierra Leone. I was at that time a Medical Technologist, working in the laboratory of our "bush" hospital at Rotifunk. Dr. Mabel Silver was the doctor. The only nurse/midwife had left not long before for furlough.

I was concerned about Dr. Silver, for the work load was too much for her, made doubly difficult because of the lack of a nurse. While we had African staff, who were very loyal, at that time the nurses had little training (more like nurses' aides). Ernest Kroma, our dispenser, was indispensable.

I knew that Dr. Silver had had a heart attack some years earlier. One evening at supper I said to her, "Dr. Silver, I think you should tell me what I should do if you should have another heart attack."

She laughed, and said she would tell me if it came to that. I reminded her that she might not be able to tell me. So she told me what injection she should have.

It was only the next day that she came home very tired late in the afternoon, after seeing four hundred patients. I was in charge of housekeeping, and gave direction to meal preparation. When supper was ready, I went to her room where she was lying down, and called her. She said, "I think it is time for that injection." She was having severe pain from an angina attack. I ran to the hospital to see our head nurse, "Mama Abby," and told her I needed her to bring the injection. I asked her not to tell anyone else what had happened. She gave the injection, and after a little while the doctor asked me to have the nurses bring over the charts for the persons in the hospital, as she wouldn't be able to go over! One did, and she got up to write orders. A little later, a Lebanese woman came to the door, saying that a young woman patient we had seen that afternoon was coughing up blood. I had not had time to report the lab findings to the doctor, so I told her then that the sputum was full of tubercle bacilli. Since the Lebanese were financially able, she told me to tell Mama Abby to go give an injection of morphine to the patient, and then tell them to take her to Freetown (the capital city) as soon as possible.

I was very concerned, because I knew that Dr. Silver could have another attack and die at any time. So I went down the hill to the railroad station, and asked the Station Master if there was a goods (freight) train coming through that night. (I knew that there were no passenger trains until the next day, and at that time there were no roads.) I explained that I must get Dr. Silver to a doctor in Freetown, and asked whether it would be possible for me

76

to take her on the train. He was very willing to make arrangements, and I went back to see Ernest Kroma. I asked him not to tell anyone else because I knew that many people would be upset if they heard that Dr. Silver was so ill, but I told him I would need him to come with some men at about 2:00 a.m. to carry her down to the train on a lawn chair we had. I then went back and told the doctor of the arrangements I had made, and said, "You will go, won't you, Doctor Silver?" She gave an answer so typical of her – that she would, because if she didn't she knew it would be an extra worry for me!

It happened that an English woman, who was teaching at our Harford School for Girls, about 20 miles away, was with us in order to have a physical exam. I asked her to help me by packing a suitcase for Dr. Silver. When she finished, she said, "I have put in a pair of white gloves, too."

I said, "Why would she need white gloves?"

Her answer, "Well, you know that in Freetown she may need to go to some official event, where she would need the gloves." It wasn't until later that I laughed about this. I am sure she had no idea of how ill the doctor was.

I was able to get into a box car with the doctor as planned, and went on the trip of 55 miles—a very slow trip. I found that the Station Master had phoned the hospital in Freetown and talked to the head nurse (who was from Rotifunk, and had known Dr. Silver since she was a child.) At about 8:00 a.m. we reached the point where the road from Freetown ended, and she herself was there with an ambulance. I of course went with them to the hospital, and then went to the town. I had had no sleep all night, and of course had been under great stress. I was glad to eat a little breakfast, have a bath, and go to bed!

Later in the day I went to see Dr. Silver, and wrote down a list of instructions. I would not be able to treat any patients (legally), and would have to send them away. We had T.B. patients in the hospital who were being treated with a new medicine. She told me the symptoms that might occur, in which case I should stop the medication. Some outpatients were taking a series of injections which she had ordered, and the dispenser and I could treat them.

I returned the next day to the hospital, where I was in charge! For the next two weeks I worked to close down the hospital. It was very difficult to send people away who had come from miles around, many of whom had no other place to go for medical treatment. To them, all white women in white uniforms were "doctors," and they could not understand why I could not treat them.

Time does not allow to tell about the child who was brought in with cerebral malaria (I confirmed that in the lab), and who died later, in spite of the treatment which we gave her (we couldn't turn her away!) I felt very bad about that.

Later, Dr. Silver recovered, and persuaded the doctor who took care of her to allow her to stay in Sierra Leone instead of returning to the States. Eventually, she came back to Rotifunk, supposedly to work part time. By then we had a new nurse from the States, and a midwife from England. Then both of them became ill with a mysterious disease which was never diagnosed—but that, too, is another story!

Although I have many pleasant memories of Sierra Leone and later Ghana, my experiences during those days are the most memorable.

Missionary Sierra Leone 1950-1962
McCurdy School, Santa Cruz, New Mexico
1966-1968
Executive Secretary North and West Africa
1968-1972
Ghana—1973-1980

Mission Interpreter Southeastern Jurisdiction
1980-1982
Mississippi-1982-89

(Transferred to Deaconess relationship 1983)
Volunteer in 5 countries in Africa—1989-1990
(Evangelical United Brethren, United Methodist)

(Submitted 2000)

My Work at the Chicago Deaconess Home

Of my many Methodist deaconess appointments, I found The Chicago Deaconess Home one of my most challenging and rewarding. I was third on the staff of three who cared for twenty retired deaconesses and missionaries.

I was the last active deaconess employed as "Visitor to Hospitalized Children Receiving Free Care." Monday through Friday I went to the hospital, helping most in pediatrics and with seniors there who were patients from our two Chicago Methodist Homes.

Mealtimes, weekends, and week days, middle afternoon and bedtime, I helped with the care of the residents. Dinner and supper were served around a long white linen-covered table, the administrator and assistant serving as hostesses. I served the food and carried food to some residents, but ate with the group and helped clear and set the table.

I assisted at bedtime and other times, taking residents to their doctors' appointments by taxi. I helped entertain—T.V., radio, storytelling, arts and crafts, holiday decorations, residents' shopping needs, etc. One afternoon a week I served as church secretary in the northwest area of the city, where many youth were on parole. I used keys to enter a high wall gate, church door and office door. On Friday evenings I helped with play night, checking for guns, knives and drugs as youth came into the gym.

I served with the children during the polio epidemic, learning to use the "Sister Kenny Method" of heat, warm water, sand bags. Other deaconesses and I visited tenements to tell mothers to go to schools and churches where sugar cube prevention clinics were held. These mothers had no newspapers or radios.

Although I went into dangerous "city jungles" and other areas to the children, youth and seniors, by the "el" subway and bus, rain or shine, summer heat of Chicago wind and winter snow, God kept me safe.

The Chicago Home for Deaconesses later became a social orientation shelter for Korean students.

Pauline "Polly" Whitacre

Deaconess U.S.A. 1945-1972
(The Methodist Church, United Methodist Church)
(Submitted 2000)

China Sky

My first trip to China as a missionary of the Methodist Episcopal Church was in December of 1931. During the first term of service overseas, I taught music theory and accompanied the choir at the Hwa Nan (South China) Girls College in Foochow. Music was an important part of the curriculum, and many girls were eager to learn. We had several pianos and a small pump organ for lessons and practice, and a missionary friend loved the mandolin and started a mandolin group.

During the late nineteen-thirties everyone was looking toward Generalissimo Chiang Kai-Chek and expecting great things of him and his followers. However, we entered the nineteen-forties in the midst of a war. As the opposing forces neared Foochow, we knew the soldiers would be coming. We had to have a safe place to send the students to get them out of harm's way. One of the U.S. missionaries went upriver and made arrangements for a second campus. There were caves, of sorts that would offer protection from bombings, and we would be away from the main road and river.

We moved the girls, their books and belongings, science equipment, library books and even a piano on river boats. I was glad to know that the students would be able to continue their lessons. As we went in river boats to the temporary campus, our boatmen often had to get out on the river bank as they pulled the boat upriver with ropes, past the rapids. We realized that the men who ran the river boats knew what they were doing. I was not afraid, just eager to get back to teaching.

Up near the new campus there was an old ancestral shrine which had been abandoned. There we put a piano for lessons because the girls could get to the shrine and safely back to their rooms, or to nearby caves, when the planes were close and the alarm sounded. For quite some time we began classes at 5:00 a.m., allowing the students to finish their schoolwork before the planes came. One day while giving a lesson I heard a plane coming. Running to the open doorway, I saw the plane close enough even to notice the pilot's goggles. As the student and I were running for shelter, I prayed that this man was a Christian who would realize this was a mission station. This second campus up the river was at Tai Ping (meaning "Peace") and there in the midst of war we found God's peace.

Eugenia Savage
Missionary China 1931-1944, Singapore 1959-1970
(Methodist Episcopal Church, The Methodist Church, U.M.C.)

(Submitted 2000)

A Community Center in Pennsylvania

I certainly remember some of the struggles and difficulties of my work in a Community Center in Harrisburg, Pennsylvania. Before I arrived the former director had sent a mimeographed sheet in which it was noted that on a street near the "Mission," as it was called, there were 108 children in one block. The street was not identified. When I arrived, I started visiting various families in their homes. I found that many of the streets were crowded with children. It took me a good two months to be sure which street and block to which the writing had referred. It was indeed near the Center.

Across the street from the Mission was a vacant area, and the neighbors let me know that the city had just demolished several buildings. One of these was "The Bucket of Blood," a beer joint. I asked why in the world it had such a name and the answer was, "There was a murder there almost every week."

One night I went to visit a home on the crowded street nearby, because the father had just been electrocuted in his own home. He had gone to the basement area to see what he could do about the electricity, which had gone off. The basement floor was only dirt, and was often muddy from water leakage. As he turned the electricity on, the water at his feet connected with the current and killed him. I sat with his wife and children and other relatives for part of the night, as was the custom in the community.

The girls in our Scout Troop could not begin to afford uniforms, and we settled for a white blouse and a dark skirt, preferably green. As Halloween approached, the Troup decided to participate in "Trick or Treat" for UNICEF. We made sure that the girls wore their uniforms, and two went together. They also knew that they were not to enter any house. As they left, I remember crying, thinking that these girls were going out to collect money for children in other parts of the world, when they had none themselves! Some came back with money, and some came back with stories of older boys who "robbed them," or with empty boxes. In their troop meeting they made the decision about how they wanted the money used. They were very definite that it should be used for "handicapped children." When I sent it off, I asked that that decision be honored.

The "Mission" has been relocated twice since those earlier years. All the area where I once worked has been remodeled as part of the Capitol grounds. Now the Neighborhood Center has a state-of-the-art building on a street in the same general area. Today it is well supported, and its program includes a Day Care Center, classes and groups for elementary students, a wonderful woodcraft shop, a chapel, and activities for older people. It has not ceased to be a "good neighbor" to its entire community area.

Helene R. Hill
Deaconess USA 1950-1986
(The Methodist Church, United Methodist Church)
(Submitted 2000)

Escape from Liberia

[The following is a letter written by Loretta Gruver, a nurse, concerning events of Sept. 8-16, 1994, when she was forced to leave Ganta, Liberia during the civil war in that country.]

Thursday, September 8, 1994—At 8:30 the military went through the streets of Ganta telling all the people to go to their houses and the students to go home from school. They announced that there was a curfew from 6:00 P.M. to 6:00 A.M. By 10:00 that morning the hospital was starting to get many seriously wounded soldiers from the fighting in Gbanga, which is 50 miles from Ganta and headquarters of Charles Taylor, the head of the NPFL (National Patriotic  Front of Liberia). Since Ganta United Methodist Hospital was the only functional hospital in Greater Liberia, we were thankful to be able to meet the needs of the patients coming to us.

Friday, September 9—More wounded came and rumors of increased fighting were many. Four Catholic sisters arrived in Ganta after walking for two days through the bush from Gbarnga.

September 10, Saturday—The hospital staff felt it best for me not to sleep on the mission because of increased rumors. They wanted me to spend the night at the Leprosy Rehabilitation Center with the Catholic sisters who had come from Gbarnga. This is about one-half mile from the mission. The border to Guinea was closed, so no one could leave. At 2:00 A.M. armed men came and demanded money, or else they would kill us. We gave them the money they wanted through an open window, and all slept in the hall where there were no windows. Throughout the night we prayed and felt God's protective hand in a real way.

September 11, Sunday—The border was still closed, so we spent all day at my house. Things were very hectic at the hospital. The staff were very faithful, but they sent their families to the bush for safety. We all slept at my house, and it was rather quiet.

September 12, Monday—Border still closed. Hospital full and busy. At about 6:00 P.M. we heard a noise and confusion from Ganta Town (about one-half mile from the mission). They were attacking Ganta and heading for the mission. The four sisters from Gbarnga and I ran though the swamp rice to the Rehab Center. We went to the back part where there are six rooms used for classes. The five of us were in one room. The other five rooms were filled with Liberians also seeking safety. At about 8:30 P.M. the soldiers came and took money from some, but did not enter our room. At 2:30 they returned, and broke all the other doors and took the people out. When they tried to break our door, it did not break. We once again felt God's hand protecting us.

September 13, Tuesday—Up at daybreak. Wanted to leave, but felt it was not safe, as the soldiers were still looking for us. At 10:30 there was a sudden silence, so we all left with one small bag each, and felt God's cloud of protection as we went back through the swamp rice and walked three miles to the border. With much hassle, $180.00, and God's protecting hand, we crossed the border with 40,000 Liberians into Guinea. Truly God's protection was felt as we reached safety. We took a taxi to Nzerekore in Guinea, about fifty miles from the border, where we were welcomed by the Catholic mission and church.

September 14, Wednesday—Registered with UNCHR to get refugee status and got cleaned up from "swamp walking." Having only the clothes we were walking out with made it necessary to get a few basic things.

September 15, Thursday—Rested and started "processing" all we had experienced. In late afternoon the Sisters and Brothers from Sanniquellie (Liberia) came looking for us. What a joy to see them! They had escaped from Liberia to Ivory Coast on September 14.

September 16, Friday—All rested and rejoiced at being alive!!!

[*This was the third time Loretta had to leave Liberia because of the war. After her escape to Guinea as described above, she returned to her home in Indiana. She was able to return to Liberia in 1998 and stayed until retirement at Brooks-Howell Home after 35 years in Liberia.*]

Loretta Gruver
Missionary Liberia 1963-1999
(The Methodist Church, United Methodist Church)
(Submitted 2000)

About 1953, Rural Tennessee

The one-room church building was adequate for worship services and meetings, but for four Sunday School classes on Sunday mornings it was a different matter. The Men's Class teacher with his booming voice could be easily heard by the men—and by the women, the youth and the children's classes. Concentration by these other class members was very difficult.

The women had failed in their efforts to get classrooms built. The men, who controlled the finances, insisted that it would be impossible to raise the money needed. (Of course, they didn't understand the problem—they could hear their teacher!)

During home visits one of the women discussed the situation with my US-2 co-worker and me. We shared with her the Lord's Acre plan, growing a cash crop to raise funds for church needs. As President of the Woman's Society of Christian Service, she decided to bring the idea to the attention of the women at their next meeting.

We were present during that meeting. One widow had a field that could be used; the president's husband and son would do the plowing and planting; another member's husband sold fertilizer, and she would speak to him. The women were sure that if the men would plow and plant they could to the "chopping" and picking, which was all done by hand in those days.

The following Sunday it was obvious that the women had talked with their husbands. The Sunday School Superintendent announced that plans were under way for a Lord's Acre cotton crop to start a building fund for classrooms. "A field has been donated by Mrs. A, so let's all work together."   Without hesitation the fertilizer, seeds and labor for plowing and planting had been donated.

Most of the able-bodied adults, youth and older children—and we Church and Community Workers—worked to hoe, and, in September, to pick the bale of cotton, which sold for $500. Soon a carpenter church member started to work. Another Lord's Acre crop was projected for the next year; but cash contributions were received which took care of the rest of the cost.

The women got no credit for instigating this effort, but their goal was accomplished—never mind the credit!

Ann McKenzie
Deaconess and Church & Community Worker
1948-1988
(The Methodist Church, United Methodist Church)
(Submitted 2001)

The Loneliest Night of My Life

It wasn't Saturday, but it was the loneliest night of the week. Actually, it was the loneliest night of my life. It was 1954. I was on a boat that had just pulled out of Montevideo, Uruguay. Three of us had left New York together, headed for our very first missionary assignments. One stayed in Rio [Rio de Janeiro, Brazil] and then we were two. One stayed in Montevideo, and then I was one!

I told myself that things would be better in the morning. After all, the dock in Rio had been flooded with well wishers, including those who had come to greet Elsie. There was even a band to welcome a returning athletic team! What a joyous reception Rio gave us. Then in Montevideo missionaries and others from Crandon were able to board ship and find us in our stateroom. Lois was warmly received. So now it was my turn.

Morning came, but there were no crowds to welcome the ship—only dock hands going about their business. The day was gray and rainy, the docks and warehouses a dreary gray. No band, no shouts of welcome. I gathered up my belongings and followed others down the gangplank and into the large building where luggage was taken. Milling crowds, looking for luggage, trying to find the proper lines, and nobody available to answer questions.

Finally, a young woman accompanied by a stately gentleman approached me. It was the Director and the Chairman of the Board from the school in Rosario [Argentina] where I was to serve. Helen explained that they weren't supposed to be there. Docks were off limits (This was during the time of Peron's presidency,) The president of the Board had managed to get them in, probably by bribing the doorkeeper. Well, I am opposed to bribery on general principles, but I must admit that I was glad to see them. Loneliness fled!

Patricia Richardson
Missionary Argentina 1954-1997
(The Methodist Church, United Methodist Church)
(Submitted 2001)

The Most Fearful Moment of My Career as a Deaconess

I was halfway through year seven of my appointment to the challenging ministries of the Wesley Community Center in Portsmouth, Virginia. Our neighboring church of historic Methodism was two blocks west and north. Our neighboring Child Service Center, a day-care operation, was two blocks west and south. Together we provided a triangular setting for multiple services. These program ministries were very important for our neighborhood, almost completely changed from Caucasian to African-American.

The Talent Show, scheduled this night for the church fellowship hall, had been moved to the community center. Our pastor, the first African-American appointed to the church, was concerned that some of the dance numbers might be inappropriate for a church setting.

The show opened, and the house was packed. The program numbers moved along. The "Jackson Five," a group of talented neighborhood youth (who looked and sounded like "The Originals") were being wildly applauded. Suddenly, there was a loud noise, sounding like gunfire, and movement toward the hallway and the front exit began.

Discovering that the noise was a brick thrown by an unhappy nonparticipant, I hastened to the front steps. I thought I could return the group and the show would continue as another staff member worked with the brick-thrower.

Outside the small auditorium, into the hallway, through the front doors and down six or eight steps, the mass-movement continued. I felt myself being swept into the crowd and moved forward by it. I had no control of where my body was going. I could feel no anger in the group, only fear. Soon the fear was enveloping me as I thought how easy it would be for us to trample each other. Would we get through this night without injuries?

Within seconds I was on the sidewalk. I could not remember placing my foot on any step, but I was in safe roller-skating territory. The crowd on the street was still moving, walking fast now or running, moving in smaller groups in homeward directions.

I walked quietly, touching every step, into the center lounge. I felt I knew more about the power of fear and crowd panic. I knew that tomorrow would bring a better day, and that in the days ahead we would more carefully plan the details of all activities.

Ruth Mayhall
Deaconess USA 1948-1986
(The Methodist Church, United Methodist Church)
(Submitted 2001)

Our Venture into Africa

My mother was well aware of my early and deep commitment to a call to mission work, but after I met Hunter and told her of our plans to be married, she very quietly remarked, "I suppose that being married to a preacher is almost the same as following your dream of overseas work." In some way she and I both knew that wasn't quite true. However, he came to Florida from Berea, met my parents, and we were later married in Danforth Chapel in Berea.

Seven years after that my parents and my brother came to New York, to see us and our five-year-old Peggy sail for England on the *Queen Mary*. My mother's joy in seeing this take place was in knowing that I had the best of two worlds, and the call I held in my heart was to be fulfilled after all.

After five days in London we boarded a combination freight-passenger ship headed for Capetown, South Africa, a sea journey of seventeen days. We waited there in the Andrew Murray Mission for about a week before our Chevrolet Suburban vehicle arrived and the real journey began.

Two "green kids with a five-year-old" made their way toward Southern Rhodesia, unaware of the total experience ahead, no road map of the American variety, but a general outline as to what places we would pass through on that 2,000 mile trip. No overnight accommodations were arranged beforehand. We would just take what we could find.

I wonder now how we could have been so relaxed with the uncertainty of it all. We drove through a desert-like area, which at that time I naively assumed might be the edges of the Kalahari, Not so, but the people were interesting, walking along the red clay dusty roads, with their bundles on their heads. This later became part of our everyday lives in Rhodesia (later Zimbabwe). We spent a night in a Johannesburg hotel which we found on our own, unaware of concern. The manager, realizing that Peggy and I waited in the car while Hunter went in to inquire about accommodations, told him to "go bring your family inside immediately."

After almost a week we arrived at Old Umtali, with a great deal of wonder about it all, to be welcomed by waiting fellow missionaries, grateful for an unseen guiding hand which has continued leading for the past fifty years since we stepped on African soil!

Beth Griffin
Missionary Southern Rhodesia (Zimbabwe)
1951-1967
(The Methodist Church)
(Submitted 2001)

My Years in Alaska

It is a long time to remember, since I was in Alaska the decade during which Alaskans voted to become a state, and I do remember some who voted against it.

Boys and girls of all ages were mixed in the Jesse Lee Home dining room seating. One youngster, I thought, was quiet and mannerly. Suddenly he pounded the table with both fists and yelled, "The winner! I finished first!"

On another day Jimmy, who was really a shy youngster, needed a Kleenex from his dresser, but he would not go get it. I told him it was O.K., we would see that his dinner was there when he returned. He would not move and I thought he was stubborn. Later I learned that his whole house and family took less room than one third of the dining room. He wasn't stubborn. He was scared to death. Thankfully, he learned that he was loved and that we would care for him.

Our summer started early, early enough each year to hide Easter eggs outside on the ground with no snow. Those bright days, not hot, lasted about four months, and how the garden did grow in that time! I learned with older boys how to transplant small cabbage plants. Those cabbages became the largest ever seen. Tourists didn't have to exaggerate. They just were that big. More than two tons of carrots were stored in the root cellar that August, for our use until the next summer.

Winters in Seward were not dark, as has been said. On clear or moonlight nights I could see persons for miles from Jesse Lee Home, down hill, to Seward or acres across Resurrection Bay to Mount Alice. But when it was cloudy with <u>no</u> snow reflection it WAS dark. Seward was not in the coldest part of Alaska, but the snow was deep and heavy. Resurrection Bay waters were just above freezing, which made it possible for large or small boats to enter and dock there the year around.

My years in Alaska were an experience and an education.

Rachel Yokel
Deaconess US 1950-1975
(The Methodist Church, United Methodist Church)
(Submitted 2001)

Memories of Afghanistan

I visited a group of aid workers in Afghanistan in May 1996. I traveled from Peshawar to Kabul by Red Cross plane. We landed on a rough airstrip and completed the entrance formalities on the tarmac by the plane. They drove us in a Red Cross station wagon along the countryside toward Kabul. It was like stepping back 2000 years in time as we saw the tents of the nomads with the animals around them. The terrain looked harsh.

As we entered the city, the destroyed buildings along the wide streets bore evidence of the warfare of the last fifteen years. The sandbags in front of the guest house and the sounds of an occasional outgoing missile flying over our heads toward the Taliban position reminded me that fighting was still in process. In May 1996 the Taliban were fighting for control. At the sound of the incoming missiles we took cover. My host knew the difference.

I remember my hostess who shared her spacious accommodation with me. She was a nurse from Finland who worked in a clinic for women and children. We had one electric light and hot water made possible by solar power. We had several types of food, but my memory is stuck on the long buns of *naan* bread that we bought in the bazaar and reheated in the home. I remember her health clinic crowded with women and children and the aid workers, who treated the whole body with medicines, teaching and recreation.

I spent many hours of conversation over our *naan* bread and green tea with two American eye specialists who were responsible for a very comprehensive eye program in the country. The young women students of the Physical Rehabilitation School, not yet under the harsh restrictions of the Taliban, enjoyed visiting with us. One-legged victims of land mines walked the streets. The boys and girls on the way to school were friendly.

I remember the 173-mile trip by road along the Kabul River and Khyber pass. The ride through the Kabul gorge was spectacular. For two hours high rocky hills of colorless rock rose up on both sides of the river, then the river gradually widened and finally became a swampy valley. After three hours we had a rest stop when we competed with each other to find the largest rock to hide behind. After that we sat on the floor in a tea shop filled with flies and drank green tea from disposable clay cups.

We stopped at Jalabad, a large laid-out city with little evidence of war. From there it was not far to the Pakistan border. Our vehicle stopped some distance from the Pakistani entrance gate. We took our baggage, quickly cleared immigration and walked through the gate as large numbers of Afghans fought with the soldiers to follow us. The soldiers harshly beat them back. Pakistan had no more room for Afghan refugees. That memory of the crowds fighting to enter Pakistan is a nightmare that often haunts me now, more than five years later.

Frances Major
Missionary India 1946-1986;
after retirement, 1987-1989
(The Methodist Church, United Methodist Church)
(Submitted 2001)

The New Lady at Wesley House

Ever since I was a child, I knew that I wanted to work with people through a settlement house. I began as a volunteer at one of the largest settlement houses in the south, Kingsley House in New Orleans, and at a Methodist settlement, St. Marks in the French Quarter of New Orleans. Then I was appointed by the old Missionary Council of the Methodist Church South to Wesley Community House in Louisville, Kentucky.

I arrived at Wesley House on Labor Day to be met by a group of five young girls sitting on the steps waiting for the "new worker." These girls seemed to be 12 to 15 years of age, all dressed in shorts, a bit embarrassed to talk to the new person that they did not even know. Frances, who seemed to be the leader, asked whether or not they could come the next day to have a club. We talked together for a few minutes as I juggled my suitcase, and we decided that they would come to the House the next day after school. They seemed to be satisfied with the answer and moved aside so that I could actually enter the House for the first time. The first Sunday in Louisville I was met by another group of girls who asked if I would take a walk with them in the afternoon after church. They met me promptly at the agreed time to walk to the Cave Hills Cemetery, which was about twenty blocks away. During the week I had been there I had learned that transportation meant walking. Even the agency did not own a car.

On the way back from the cemetery, I heard two or three girls back of me discussing who would ask their important question. I turned around to find out what they wanted to know. They had been discussing whether or not we could stop for an ice cream cone at the drug store. I realized that one of the youngsters, Sue, was the preacher's daughter, so I inquired whether or not she was allowed to buy things on Sunday. Sue told me that she was not allowed to spend her money on Sunday, but that Mary Katherine would treat her today and she would treat Mary Katherine in turn tomorrow. Apparently, this system had worked before.

Years later it is interesting to get letters from people who were part of the services of Wesley House as members as well as the students from the University and two seminaries who did internships. One of the letters in 2001 was from a former student who had been appointed to the agency to work with small children, but soon learned that she preferred to work with older youngsters. In so doing, she found her own ministry with the Baptist Church in Brazil. Another letter came from a former member who had spent a week at the agency camp before she entered the monastery to become a Catholic nun. Dorothy's letter stated that she was retired but still working to change some of the laws of Kentucky to assure quality teaching was done in home schools.

Every year the memories come back of time at Wesley House when a group of sixteen to twenty friends come to see me at Brooks-Howell. The women in the group were members of a supper club when they were teen-agers. They were married; they brought their children; they have become a three-generational club.

When I went up the steps that day with my suitcase, not knowing anyone in Louisville, Kentucky, how could I have known that the years would bring so many happy days?

(This vignette was taken from an interview of Helen Mandelbaum by Ann Janzen.)

Helen Mandelbaum
Deaconess USA 1938-1979
Volunteer work with the National Division
for 10 years
(The Methodist Church, United Methodist Church)
(Submitted 2002)

How Two Churches Were Built

Many memories of experiences in Brazil flood my mind, but the one I want to tell about is the last pastoral appointment I received. A phone call came one day from the Bishop. (At one time he was a young man in a church I served. Now he was my bishop!) He said that I could choose between two cities for my next appointment. Martha and I chose the city of Belo Horizonte. (She would also receive a new appointment.) Annual Conference was in January.

Severe flooding slowed the moving process of the pastors, so it was late February before we finally moved. I was to pastor a congregation known as Barreiro. They were unhappy and a group had left to join the Assemblies of God, saying the congregation was dead. Before I got there another group left, saying the congregation was too Pentecostal! When I arrived only a dozen people were left.

We met in a small storefront type building on a large lot. The congregation began to grow and we had dreams of putting up a new church building. At one service I told the people, "Last night in a dream I saw our new church. It was full of people praising God!"

They all exclaimed, "That is a good sign, pastor!" Some money was slowly being raised and we hired an architect to draw up plans for a new temple. He examined our lot, took measurements, and listened to our needs. Months later he came to show us the preliminary blueprints. The church he envisioned for us was spacious, practical and beautiful. Everyone liked it, but when the probable cost was known they lost hope. "Oh, pastor, how can we ever do that?" they asked.

I replied, "Have you forgotten my dream?"

Soon it was time for our three-month home assignment and itineration. One Sunday we spoke at Central United Methodist Church in Walla Walla, Washington. After we had shown our slides, a young couple chatted with us, saying, "We are inspired by your message and we will be praying for you."

Back in Brazil we continued construction on two church buildings, since Martha's church was also building. But by year's end Advance Special funds were running out. About Christmas time a phone call came from the young man in Walla Walla. He asked how the construction was going. I told him we were ready to put roofs on two buildings but were out of funds. He wanted to know how much it would cost to finish the two churches.. Off the top of my head I replied, "It will take at least $100,000." He said, "We will keep you in mind."

Can you imagine our surprise when he gave exactly that amount? The buildings were completed. In 1993 the Barreiro church was dedicated with 180 members. The pastor who followed me was a former seminary student of mine. Under her leadership the church experienced several years of rapid growth. When we returned to Brazil for a visit in 1999, the pastor insisted that I preach at Barreiro. My heart was beating pretty fast as we approached the building in a friend's car.

Soon I was surrounded by many old friends. The people who were teen-agers during my ministry were now married and introduced me to their spouses and babies. As I preached more than 300 people filled the sanctuary and balcony to capacity. At the close of the service the pastor made an appeal and thirteen people came forward to accept Christ. Even now tears of joy fill my eyes as I remember that day. God is good!

Leon Strunk
Missionary Brazil 1950-1953, 1958-1991
Volunteer in Brazil 1992-1998
(The Methodist Church, United Methodist Church)
(Submitted 2002)

Fire!

I have many happy memories of my twenty-seven years as teacher at Red Bird Mission High School, but I also have some sad ones. God was always at work in the bad as well as the good times.

One of my most vivid and unforgettable memories is of May 18, 1981, the day after Red Bird High School's graduation. I went to the school earlier than anyone else because I had English notebooks to grade. I never reached my classroom on the second floor because when I walked into the building I discovered that it was on fire. I rushed out of the building and started spreading the news of the fire. But being a creature of habit, I conscientiously locked the door of a burning building when I left it. (The absurdity of that action did not hit me until some time later.)

The wooden building built in the early 1920s burned very rapidly. Fire trucks came from as far as forty miles away, but there was little they could do except try to save the surrounding buildings. We were able to save the historic Beverly Church on one side of the school by pouring water on it for hours, but we were unable to save the gymnasium near the school on the other side.

Community people came to help move materials out of the mobile classrooms and paint from a nearby paint shop. Staff and three generations of Red Bird students were grieving over the loss of our school, but we were also thanking the Lord that there were no students in it.

Before the fire was completely out, the Rev. Ed Ehresman, the Director of Red Bird Mission, said, "We will start school in August." His faith and hope inspired the rest of us. Thus began a very hectic summer of putting our faith into action.

The news of the fire spread quickly, and help came from the local community and from United Methodists across the country. Local groups and individuals provided temporary buildings and labor to move and set them up. Also, any available spaces in the church campgrounds and the girls' dorm that could be converted into classrooms, offices or cafeteria were utilized. United Methodists from all over the country came with work teams and materials to help. Countless numbers provided financial and prayer support.

Since our library had been destroyed in the fire, we had to create a new library that would meet state and Southern Association accreditation requirements before school started in August. Books came from everywhere and volunteers appeared to help catalog and shelve them in one of our temporary buildings. We met the minimum requirements, and books continued to arrive throughout the year.

Several people suddenly found a use for those musical instruments they had in storage. With donated instruments and a renovated camp cabin, we had a music department.

Because of all the hard work, we were ready for the opening date of school. Some of us were still scrubbing and waxing the floors in our four-room temporary building the weekend before the opening of school. We began classes with only the teachers having textbooks, but that was soon remedied.

For the next two years we were in our unique school with classrooms scattered all over the mountainside. Students were very cooperative in getting to classes on time. The fact that we could see our new school being constructed down in the valley compensated for any inconveniences we had. Our blueprints for a new school that had been on hold suddenly had to be put into use.

The events of the summer of 1981 reinforced our appreciation for being a part of the connectional system of The United Methodist Church.

Bettie Sue Smith
U.S. 2, Deaconess
Allen High School 1957-1971,

Red Bird Mission 1971-1998
(The Methodist Church, United Methodist Church)
(Submitted 2002)

His Mysterious Ways

 February is the month of entrance examinations all over Japan. It often snows and even develops into a blizzard in the worse case, causing great predicaments for the examinees. It was one such day in 1945, when at age 12 I took an entrance exam for a high school, my mother's alma mater and the most prestigious in the prefecture. To my dismay, I failed. In fact, the result was only to be expected. Just two months before I, my mother and two younger brothers evacuated from Tokyo to my mother's hometown, Hirosaki, the most northern part of the island. The previous year until then I had little time for study, let alone prepare for the entrance examination. Most of my time was spent in a bomb shelter either at home or at school, avoiding the B-29 raids. Thus, I grudgingly entered a Methodist girls' high school. It was but a second choice for me.

Hirosaki is a city with a strong Protestant background. It produced the first Methodist bishop in Japan. Yet, I had never been directly exposed to Christianity until I entered this school, just as a majority of my classmates had never been. The local pastor's once-a-month harangue at chapel was an ordeal. On the other hand, I was fascinated by abridged stories of the Old Testament I read in the library—stories of the serpent's temptation, the forty days' inundation, the sibling rivalry, strange dreams, the Red Sea split into two, etc. etc.

During the six years of my high school days a number of missionaries would come and go. Among them were austere Miss Byler, who taught me the importance of punctuality, and gentle Miss Brittain, who encouraged me to go on to higher education. They both looked ancient, though they must not have been any older than I am now. The most memorable missionaries were the J-3s (Japan Threes) fresh out of college. Especially Miss Hartley and her Bible class after school were very popular. It had strong magnetism even for college boys around the city. This worried the older missionaries. Finally, Miss Hartley was transferred to the most southern end of Japan. I still remember her swollen eyes full of tears when she gave a heart-rending farewell message in front of the whole school gathered in the auditorium. How indignant and sad we students were for her.

I received baptism before I graduated from this Methodist Girls' High School. It was the beginning of my new life. Indeed, He works in mysterious ways.

Fusako Kudo Krummel
Missionary Japan 1967-1999
(The Methodist Church, United Methodist Church)
(Submitted 2002)

Memories of Sue Bennett College

During my twenty-seven years at Sue Bennett College in Kentucky many events stand out in my memory. Two of these follow:

Dorothy Marie Watson was the sponsor of the education club and I sponsored the Christian clubs. Members of these clubs decided jointly to sponsor a tutoring program for elementary children living in a low income housing project, using the community room of the project as a meeting place. A couple of our students obtained some large boxes from a funeral home and made dividers around the tables to provide privacy and to discourage interchange between tables. A few years later one of the young girls who had been tutored enrolled in Sue Bennett as an entering freshman.

Another memorable experience occurred in the spring of the early 1970s. Asbury College had experienced a "spontaneous revival" and a few Asbury students came down to Sue Bennett one evening to tell us of their experiences here. After the supper hours they met in the auditorium with some of our students and a couple of faculty members. A time of quiet prayer, led by students, lasted until around 2:00 a.m. Some of our students would go to the dorms, wake up fellow students, and bring them to the meeting for prayer.

A week later at the 10:00 weekly chapel service this spirit continued, spearheaded by our own students. The service lasted into the next class period and on into the lunch hour. (President Hays ordered class and lunch bells turned off until the service came to an end.) We saw our students mature in faith right before our eyes, and the rest of the school year was different as students became concerned for one another. It was a quiet reaching out for a relationship deeper than they had known before. It was beautiful!

All of this was untouched by faculty; we simply watched. They were doing fine without us!

Jewel Brown
Commissioned Deaconess 1961
New England Deaconess Hospital, MA 1963-1964
Holding Institute, Texas 1964-1966
Sue Bennett College, KY 1960-1963; 1966-1990
(The Methodist Church, United Methodist Church)
(Submitted 2002)

Missionary Adventures

No rain clouds from the south, no unpleasant palm-bending winds from the north, just one of the beautiful dawns that could make living in Santa Cruz worth remembering. In those days more than a quarter of a century ago this city in eastern Bolivia was an unpaved frontier on the edge of a vast vanishing jungle. Missionaries, local preachers, often moonlighting as teachers, physicians and nurses arose each day committed to reach out to pioneer settlers with the Gospel, highlighted by arts of health and learning. While Jayne got the children ready for school, I grabbed the makings of a lunch, then headed for the jeep.

The schedule included picking up Augusto Roman, the Bolivian education supervisor, to travel some fifty miles north, visit several homesteads, and hold church committees and teachers' planning sessions. We were to end the day at a charge conference some five miles east of the last one-room schoolhouse. The better traveled road made a Y on which we took the left fork. I had previously explored a lumber track that crossed the top of the Y. As the birds began to seek their nests we headed into the bush for our last assignment.

Then, naturally, that best-laid plan ran into the unexpected. Surrounded by thick jungle, the jeep suddenly stopped its advance, but surprisingly wouldn't retreat either. The motor purred reassuringly, but our four wheels were locked. We opened the doors to the neighborhood of twilight mosquitoes, looked about, checked under the hood, swatted the swarm, while puzzlement ceased our brows.

Finally, Augusto saw that we were straddling a fallen log; the under bolts had hung on some of the holes in the *motacu* palm tree. We actually had to jack the car as dark doubled the trouble. It took both of us jumping on the log to dislodge the bolts and then drag it from under the chassis. When we finally reached the small church, Pastor David Torres and family had turned in for the night. The charge conference has yet to come to order.

LeGrand Smith
Missionary Bolivia 1952-1973 Uruguay 1977-1981,
Argentina 1982-1991
New Mexico 1974-1977
After 1991 Special Assignments NY, Bolivia,
Argentina
(The Methodist Church, United Methodist Church)
(Submitted 2002)

The Example of Connectionalism's Power
—as seen at Allen High School

[Allen High School, going back to its early days in late 19th century (1887—Woman's Home Missionary Society of the Methodist Episcopal Church), from its beginning was known, respected and a model in the Asheville community. It was a boarding and day school for black girls.]

A long-planned for dream came true on a rainy November day when thirty-eight Allen Choir members, accompanied by the principal, Julia Titus (deceased), Troy Conference home missionary Carol Chaney and Winifred Wrisley, music teachers, started toward Troy Conference [Methodist Church] on a Trailways bus. We were scheduled to take part in fifteen services of worship by music and spoken word, over thirteen days, November 9-20, 1963. From a setting of "Let All the World in Every Corner Sing" to a closing unison Kagawa poem, "Discovery" about God ". . . using my hand," we witnessed to our faith through music, words and lives, developing friendships and sharing multi-racial and intergenerational experiences throughout Troy Conference from Albany and Schenectady to the Canadian border in Swanton, Vermont. Following our final program we again climbed into the bus in the rain, and at 1:00 a.m. obeyed our loyal bus driver as he insisted that we climb the steps to the Lincoln Memorial to reflect on those days in the glow of Lincoln's face. Finally reaching Allen's parking lot on Friday afternoon, we learned that President Kennedy had been shot and had died in Dallas.

Looking back and catching up with reality, as we caught up on school work and wrote thank-you letters to each host family, we found that we had money left over—and decided unanimously to buy three <u>new</u> Everett studio pianos for the school.

Winifred Wrisley
Deaconess U.S.A. Allen High School 1955-1968,
Harwood School, New Mexico, 1968- 1974;
Special Appointment, Vermont 1975-1988
(The Methodist Church, United Methodist Church)
(Submitted 2003)

I Want a Brother

Before I went to Africa, I told my mother that I wanted a brother; but she said that was impossible, that there was no question of that, and that she wasn't going to have another baby. But she did! When the baby was being born, my father was expecting another girl, but it was a boy! He told mother that if it was a girl, she, my sister, and I would have to leave the house. After that my mother never spoke to my father.

There were twenty years between John and me. When he was four years old I left for the Congo, where I served for seven years before I left for the first time. I went to study at Scarritt College in 1958. In 1960 I returned to the Congo, and my brother was the one who always wrote to me.

The revolution started after I had been in the Congo for six months. I stayed two years, and then went back to Belgium, but I had been there only three or four months when it became possible for me to return to the Congo. My mother had promised John that he could go to visit me there, but because of the revolution it was impossible. After about six months I had to go back to Belgium again because the revolution continued, and I was a Belgium citizen.

After a couple of months I went in October to the United States. I got a job as a nurse right away in Tampa, where I stayed for nine years. In 1964 my mother and my brother came to the U.S.A., because John had completed his obligatory military service. John wanted to study in a computer school, so he did, and graduated. Father followed mother right away after she came. He didn't mind that she didn't speak to him. John got work right away in Tampa after graduating. My father was retired when he came. I kept working there as a nurse until I moved to Brooksville, Florida, where I continued nursing. My parents and John stayed in Tampa. Mother died in 1976 and father in 1984. John is still a lifelong friend for me.

I retired in Brooksville in 1990, but continued to live there until I came to Brooks-Howell in 1999. It was my sister who brought me here and made the arrangements for me to come. I am happy here. And John is coming to visit me tomorrow! [At the time she dictated this article.]

Simmone Van Ooteghem (as told to Helen L. Hill)
Missionary Congo 1950-1959
(The Methodist Church, Belgium and US)
(Submitted 2003)

Dreaming

The Bible tells that young men see visions and old men shall dream dreams. Being eighty-four years old, I have dreamed dreams.

I dreamed of having a high-steepled church that might suggest how much we think of God. Instead He gave me the porch of Dona Francisca's home as an altar and the sandy streets in front of her house as aisles which reached to the Atlantic Ocean, the heavens for a dome, the Southern Cross as a background, and for pews, each worshiper bringing his or her chair or box, while the children sat on the sandy streets.

I dreamed of constructing great, modern impressive buildings to "The Glory of God"; instead, He showed me the growth of faith in the lives of neglected people, changing their fatalistic attitudes to "I can do all things in Him who strengthens me" or "I have found resources in myself, whatever the circumstances."

I dreamed of having a great choir and a very capable, dedicated choir director; instead, He gave me Agnes, my wife playing a portable pump organ, and a choir of fishermen and their families whose music harmonized with the wind of the sea and the clap of the waves.

I dreamed of influencing governments and nations to help a needy world; instead, He gave me the knowledge that broken homes can be mended, sad lives were becoming happy, despondent people were being filled with hope, complacent young people were becoming fervent crusaders for a new heaven and a new earth, and barefooted children were learning to sing joyfully.

I dreamed of a church with a competent Director of Christian Education, beautiful classrooms, the latest equipment, the finest literature; instead He gave me my wife, teaching more than a hundred children from the small houses and huts on the narrow streets to sing "Jesus Loves Me, This I Know," and "Little Feet, Be Careful."

I dreamed of organizing programs that would feed a hungry world and of hearing the response of thankful governments; instead, I had the privilege of seeing the delighted and thankful smiles on the faces of small undernourished children as buns were given them in Vacation Bible School.

I dreamed of preaching to well-dressed, well-nourished, important, successful people; instead He gave me congregations of which many were wondering when the next daily bread would come or where the next job would be found.

I dreamed of having a very comfortable car, an impressive one; instead, He gave me a sixteen-year-old Willys, which carried me to people many of whom had never owned a pair of shoes.

I dreamed of being able to attend great concerts among my own people; instead, He gave me the opportunity of hearing choruses of children yelling joyfully as they ran to meet us: "Here come the Americans!"

William (Will) Rogers, Jr.

Missionary Brazil 1939-1963
(The Methodist Church)
(Submitted 2003)

He Learned His Lesson Too Late

My first Deaconess appointment was Wesley Community House in Key West, Florida. We worked mainly with people who had recently arrived from Cuba. A lot of the adults did not speak much English, but most of the children picked up English pretty quickly.

A lot of people in our neighborhood (we lived in the community house) had birds for pets. My house mate and I decided it would be nice to have a parakeet. She could take him to Kindergarten in the morning and I could take him to club groups in the afternoon. We called our pretty new bird "Perky." We tried to teach him to talk. I even bought a Parakeet Teaching Record. It repeated words like "hello, goodby . . . " over and over. We played it for him during times we didn't have people around.

One of my responsibilities was a girl's sewing class. Most of the girls attended the Catholic intermediate school, so when they needed my help with their sewing, they would call "Sister" or sometimes, "Miss Merritt." Although I always took Perky with me to classes and clubs at the Community House for six years, Perky never opened his mouth except to squawk or squeak.

After my work at Key West I entered the graduate School of Social Work in Cleveland, Ohio. Soon after my first semester started, I had a letter from the new worker at Key West. She said that Perky, the Parakeet, was driving them crazy because he was always yelling "Sister, Miss Merritt, Come here." Unfortunately, he learned his lesson too late!

Arlene Merritt
Deaconess USA 1952-1989
(In Japan 1981-1982)
(The Methodist Church, United Methodist Church)
(Submitted 2003)

Freezing in Peru

"Are we going to get there in time?" one of the girls asked.

"We'll have to run across the field instead of going by the road," I answered.

"But you're the one who told us not to run at 12,500 feet above sea level. We could get *saroche* (an illness caused by lack of oxygen at high elevation): came the comment of another youth.

There was no alternative; either we ran at that elevation or we would miss the one train that would take us back to Cerro de Pasco, the mining town where we were staying.

Suddenly it happened, just as I feared. In the field there were water channels we would have to cross. The water was more than icy cold. It was murder. But the alternative was worse. It would mean trying to find a place to stay overnight in the middle of nowhere. So across the ditches we plunged, with soaking and freezing feet, but thanks be to God, we reached the train station just before the train pulled in.

What were we doing up at 12,500 feet? As Christian Education Coordinator for the Peruvian Methodist Church, I had been challenging the youth in Lima to do outreach ministry. That summer for two weeks ten young people and I were carrying on two Daily Vacation Bible School on the high plateau near Cerro de Pasco, where we were staying overnight and having breakfast and supper.

At noon each day we would catch the Huancayo train to go to the isolated area where the other DVBS was held, have lunch with a family of the church, have DVBS for two hours, and then catch the train on its way from Huancayo to Lima. That day I mentioned above we had been doing special crafts with the children and just forgot the time.

Was it worth the freezing, crossing the icy ditches, eating cold food and freezing at night as well? Yes, it was. It meant joy and excitement for the children living in isolated areas without any fun things to do. It meant bringing materials for continued Sunday School with the childen, and some in-service training for the older brothers and sisters in the church who had promised to continue ministering to the children. It meant for our Lima young people the opportunity to experience the reality of the areas of greatest need in Peru, and brought them to greater commitment to the One who came not to be served but to serve. And it meant to me a new awareness of the ministry that God had and continues to do to "the least of these my brothers and sisters."

Patricia Riddell

Latin America: short-term missionary to
Argentina 1957-1959,
Woman's Division missionary to Peru 1960-1973
Mexico, 1973-1992
(with eight months in Sierra Leone & Liberia in
1979, working on curriculum for the Sunday Schools);
retired from Mexico 1992
1993, Mission Interpreter in Residence in
Southeastern Jurisdiction, UMC
(The Methodist Church, United Methodist Church)
(Submitted 2003)

A Deaconess on a Motorcycle

 I remember when I became a deaconess, but I never thought that on this day I would be writing an article on what I remembered. After having been on the college campus for a number of years, I decided to buy a small motorcycle. It was a red Honda. What fun it was from the moment it appeared on campus! And how the students enjoyed it. Every afternoon about the time for me to leave the office I was waited on by students. Each wanted to ride with me around the parking lot. They loved for the Dean of Women to take them on a ride. And the Dean loved it as much as they did! On Hallowe'en I dressed for the occasion and paraded in the campus event. I will never forget this fun and happiness for me as well as for the students.

Let's move to another event that I remember. This was during the war years. A request had come from the Federal and State governments to conserve energy. A notice was sent that lights in the halls during certain hours would be turned off. The first time they were turned off, the lights were back on in just a few minutes. When I confronted the person responsible, she responded by saying that her canary needed light. She threatened to write a letter reporting me to the "powers that be." As far as I know, no report was ever written.

I must let you know that professors are not always as smart as they believe themselves to be. One person, when talking with a personal friend of mine, said to her that he couldn't understand Mary Bethea's leaving the college campus and going to a retirement home to live with old people, and even more, sit on the porch and rock with them. What a concept he had of what retirement is like! I think he needed to come and visit a retirement community, stay a few days, and maybe get a different opinion.

Mary Bethea
Deaconess USA 1958-1991
(The Methodist Church, United Methodist Church)
(Submitted 2004)

Memories of a Deaconess

With the Christmas holidays just past, I have been recalling some of my early Christmases as I was growing up in Madison, Georgia. Those Christmas memories, in a loving family, are very pleasant ones. After having our own Christmas at home, the family (Mother, Father, younger brother Leonard and I), made our way up the street to Grandmother Thompson's. After some time enjoying Christmas with her, we went on to an aunt's for Christmas dinner, and then bundled into the car to go to my maternal grandmother's for supper, which was almost as big as dinner. On the way, my brother and I tussled over the lap robe in the back seat, pulling it back and forth!

One special Christmas stands out, when my grandfather had a carpenter build a good-sized play house for me! It had a chimney, a stove that really cooked, cast-iron skillets, furniture built for the house – including a dining room table! – and a baby bed for my doll. The doll was almost as big as I was, and really not very "cuddly!" My mother even cooked on the stove one summer. I was not allowed to make a fire in the stove unless an adult was present. The house made a nice study and "get away" place for me, with its front porch, flowers and even a back door.

As I was growing up, I was often sick. My father wasn't sure I would be able to go to school, but I persisted between bouts of illness, and graduated from Madison High School in 1926. Over the next years, I attended various nearby colleges, as health permitted. I was determined to finish college, since everyone in our family had college degrees. When I was encouraged to apply to be a deaconess, I doubted that I could pass the physical exam. However, I did, and was thrilled to be consecrated a deaconess in March 1939, right here in Asheville, at Central Church, shortly before my graduation from Scarritt College.

My work appointments took me first to Alabama and then to Louisiana as a Rural (Church and Community) Worker. In the Huntsville District, I served in a little school, and was on a circuit. On my first "5th Sunday" there (the only time some of the small churches had preaching), I asked to accompany the pastor to a small church in one of the fishing villages. There were only three in the congregation that day, two girls, eleven and thirteen, and an older man. The little girls, with their keen interest, kept drawing me back. The older one (Pat Forman) kept in contact for many years, as she went on to school, and eventually served as a missionary to Africa with Beth and Hunter Griffin. There were several other girls who were an inspiration during those years, and who went on to accomplish much. I thanked the Lord that I could be an instrument in finding them and helping them get started.

I have many memories of working in out of the way places in the hills of Alabama and the bayous of Louisiana. As a rather retiring person, I often worked behind the scenes. It didn't matter to me who got the credit, so long as things got done. I found my real talent was in identifying and developing leaders, so in many, many ways, my work lives on. Illness (back problems and migraine headaches) continued to plague me during my working years. I have memories of many hills I couldn't climb, but as I prayed for strength, with God's help, I climbed them! During those years I never really took a vacation, since times off provided the needed rest and recuperation to get back to the work I loved.

In Louisiana, I remember working with the American Indians, including helping to start a school. Not many others were working with them at that time. I also worked with the Cajuns (French Arcadians) in the bayous. While there I remember a State Extension Worker who helped out, who was also an excellent "rural worker."

A very special remembrance is the close friendship I enjoyed with Virginia (Mrs. Glenn) Laskey, well-known for her leadership in the Woman's Society of Christian Service. (Mrs. Laskey was President of the Woman's Division immediately prior to church union.) I continue to be in touch with her daughter. I especially remember some of the rejections Virginia faced, including some from her own church, because of her stands for and work toward integration and racial justice, and the strength she showed. Those same principles were important in guiding my own work.

After my time as a Rural Worker, I served as Director of Christian Education at First Church, Decatur, Georgia. (The pastor at that time was Bevel Jones, later to be Bishop). After retiring, I continued to be active in the church, which soon was to celebrate its 150th anniversary. On relatively short notice, I was asked to suggest plans for a year of celebration. I drew up a plan, and was delighted when all but one of the suggestions became reality. Several of the young adults in the church took an active part, and eight of those families have remained close friends. I have even been "honorary grandmother" in four weddings!

On my 92nd birthday, one Brooks-Howell friend wrote to me, encouraging me to come to Brooks-Howell. Another called with the same encouragement. Shortly after that, I called Thelma McGraw – and then things moved quickly. I was so thrilled to be coming here, and am delighted to be part of the Brooks-Howell family.

–Recorded and written by Elaine Gasser

Elizabeth Thompson
Deaconess USA 1939-1968
(The Methodist Church)
(Submitted 2004)

Memories of India

On nights when sleep eludes me, memories of India unlock my guarded heart and I am abed on the Bulandshahr mission Bungalow roof, counting stars while breathing the nighttime fragrance of jasmine. Drums throb in the distance, occasionally being eclipsed by shouts in the mango grove where night birds threaten the harvest. In the morning, the joyous spring festival will begin when everyone will be free to throw colored water on one another and, for once, wives may beat their husbands. Tomorrow night the *Holi* drums will boom by bonfires as men dance on them under the full moon.

On Easter morning at 4:30 a.m. I join the Bride School students in a candle lit procession on the front lawn. The next year in Ghaziabad I am alone in the peaceful grapefruit garden until Grand Trunk Road fills with *tongas* and bicycles, buses and *rickshas,* and many pedestrians. Church service will not be until afternoon. Boarding an eastbound bus, I watch for Bishvasi's village and dismount to scuff through soil, weeds, and grass clumps to the house/school where she sits with several of her school children, cooking sweets to celebrate our Holy Day. One of the boys asks Jesus to bless the food before we eat. He is not yet Christian.

On Christmas afternoon in Bulandshahr, under a brilliant blue sky, everyone on the small compound (Christian, Muslim, Hindu), men, women and children, finds a place to sit on the rug spread over the grass by the well. Fragrant rose bushes enclose us on three sides,

111

tall poinsettias on the fourth. We sing and pray before Father Christmas arrives with some little thing for everyone. Then Khalil brings buckets of hot tea and trays of warm *pakoras* and syrupy *jalebis* from the kitchen. We eat and celebrate together.

In Delhi I stroll beneath Royal Palms in the green oasis beyond Kashmiri Gate. In 1948 refugees camped here. Now, even the clamor and confusion of the nearby bazaar are muted. Later I wend my way through crowded Chandni Chauk, marveling at displays of silks and handicrafts in the shops.

In Hyderabad I sit in the garden beside the lotus pool and then wander along the lake where a soft fragrant breeze dispels the disquiet of mind and soul following conference meetings.

Near Ghaziabad I ride my bicycle westward from a village on Hapur Road as a reddish, purplish haze obscures the horizon and silhouetted bare Neem trees testify to survivability. Tomorrow, groups of Christian village school children will gather here for a Music Festival. Their laughter and joyous singing will testify to the survivability of a Faith.

In the mountains I trudge fourteen miles (three miles of which are like stairs cut into the stone), up and up to Rohtung Pass. The wind bites. There are patches of snow to avoid as we pass lone shepherds in short woolen coats, smoking their bubbling pipes and smiling at us.

On Christmas Eve I join a village pastor and his congregational leaders sitting around a charcoal heater in a mud brick room. A bucket of hot Indian tea soothes our vocal cords as we sing songs welcoming our Lord. My ailing throat gives out and I retire to the parsonage where the pastor's wife massages me with garlic, mustard and other oils until I sleep. In the following June her little David dies of typhoid fever and we weep together.

There is no end to the memories and they do not bring sleep as one lives again more deeply and intensely than ever before or since, bombarded with color as well as squalor, riches and poverty, entrancing tunes as well as clamor, irresistible delicacies and repulsive concoctions, genuine sacrificial Christianity along with an immeasurable need for the gospel.

Memories of India do not bring sleep–only yearning.

Lois Biddle Mohansingh
Missionary India 1955-1961;
(married Samuel Mohansingh 1963);
1963-1965; 1974-1977
(The Methodist Church, United Methodist Church)
(Submitted 2004)

Rocky Memories

As I place a thin chain about my neck, fingering the smooth cool rock pendant now hanging some eight inches below my chin, I think of my younger daughter, in the second or third year of her life, sitting on my lap sucking the irregularly shaped fragment and wondering how snowflakes could have been captured in its midnight blue core. What a gift her snippet of memory gave me when she recently recalled these times to me. To be certain that a child truly remembers the warm affection which surrounded her at that moment . . . I am deeply touched. All three of my children remember different moments, as we recall together several of the polished slices of agate, jade, flint, or bloodstone which I then chose to wear instead of multiple strings of beads which could so easily break when grabbed by grubby little fists.

For me, the rocky pendant also sparked related memories of hot dry days and family outings when, armed with hammers, we searched dry river banks in Central India for those misleadingly common lumps of dull rough rock which when cracked open reveal tiny magical caverns of crystalized amethyst, lavender, gold, pink and white. There were other treasures as well: dark green bloodstone splashed with coral or darker crimson, flint nodules sharply splintered, gem-streaked fragments freshly split, revealing surprising inclusions hidden for eons in the sandy, stony rocks carried from one place to another during India's Monsoon floods, when the river beds and fallow fields receive annual soaking fertilization. The sharp blows of hammers, the cries of wonder, the rush of little legs over the gravel as the young explorers hurry to show off their enchanting discoveries. We needed no Disney World to find magic during the holidays with our family, and usually another family or two, in the India of thirty years ago.

Now the children are grown, and their special rocky treasures stand on shelf-edges, or in baskets, or glass jars filled with water to brighten their colors. Learning to look at rocks, their own little ones often fill their pockets with smooth pebbles, or keep them in special little boxes. But they can catch a tiny glimpse of their parents/Rocky Adventures in India only when they break open a purchased "geode" hidden in the toes of their stockings at Christmas. With one blow they shatter the mystery, and ask for a family visit to Asheville

Gem Museum, or a stopover at one of the several tourist-inspired gem mines which dot the edges of the road they travel from Durham/Chapel Hill on a visit to grandma at Brooks-Howell Home.

Naomi Gleason Wray
Missionary India 1953- 1956
(Married Fred Wray 1956)
1958-1993
(The Methodist Church, United Methodist Church)
(Submitted 2004)

Memories Are So Beautiful

I Have So Many!

One day I was calling in our community and found a little boy who needed kindergarten. His mother said, "I would love for him to go, but he has no clothes better than what he has on."

I said, "If I can find clothes, would you let him come?"

"Oh, yes."

I found the clothes, three complete sets, shoes and socks. Joy filled their hearts when they saw what we had. I said, "All you do is keep them clean, and be there every day."

The next morning he arrived and looked as if he had been waxed and polished. He walked and looked around, amazed. During the morning I gave them story books to look at. Mickey got the prettiest one. He went off by himself, lay down on the floor and leafed through the book. Suddenly it was, "God dang; did you ever see anything so pretty!" No, I did not correct him; he had seen beauty. Kindergarten would take care of the word.

The days passed, and Mickey grew and grew–a whole new world had opened. On the closing day the house was full for a closing program. Mickey's parents were there, beaming.

After the program was over, the mother said, "Mickey has come home each day and made us learn the songs, and told us the stories–and we loved it."

I said, "Mrs. Brown*, I couldn't have done anything if the Lord and United Methodist Women had not provided our McCarty Settlement House."

She said, "Our home is better. Mickey is happy. You tell those women I said thanks, for kindergarten has been a blessing to all of us, and we can all talk to the Lord."

*Not her real name

Helen Carter
Deaconess USA
Probationary service June 1940-June 1942
Licensed 1942 –1975
(The Methodist Church, United Methodist Church)
(Submitted 2004)

Memories of Harford School

So many memories flood in while trying to pick out a few to include from ten wonderful years teaching at Harford School for Girls in Sierra Leone between 1954 -1964. Among the earliest memories is the lush beauty of the country, and the friendliness and warmth of a peaceful people. The acting principal at the time, Miriam Faust, said, as part of her early orientation, "If you're ever out walking in the evening, and you hear footsteps behind you, don't be concerned. It's probably someone following to be sure you're okay." That was Sierra Leone in 1954, and during most of those ten years.

Another highlight was the excitement leading up to Independence in 1961. More than all the political speeches or lavish celebrations, I remember the time just before midnight on April 26, 1961. Harford School students and teachers joined the townspeople and government officials of Moyamba in walking up to the playing field in town, where the British Union Jack waved over the crowd in the lights erected for the occasion. After speeches and well-wishes, at the stroke of midnight, the British flag was lowered, and the new green, white and blue Sierra Leone flag was raised to the cheers of the crowd and the strains of the new Sierra Leone National Anthem.

Memorable as all of those events were, the one that stands out most is of an older man standing in the shadows near the fence, holding his walking stick. As everyone else cheered and sang, he pounded his stick on the ground, and, over and over, quietly said to himself in tones of wonder, "**Freedom! Freedom! Freedom!**"

One of my greatest joys at Harford School was directing the school choir. For a number of years, led by then Principal June Hartranft, the choir had won the national singing competition in Freetown among several of the Girls' Secondary School Choirs from across the country. When June went on leave, I was asked to fill in – while several commiserated with the girls over their new, "green" director. We practiced – and practiced – **and practiced** the music assigned to all the schools for the competition! The British District Commissioner agreed to accompany us, and spent much of his "free" time practicing with us. Shortly before the competition he was moved to Freetown as Aide-de-Camp to the Governor, but agreed to meet us at the site of the competition in time for our appearance. Unfortunately, we failed to tell him all the choirs were singing the same number! He came to the concert hall, heard the number being sung, thought he was late, and, as he said, "slunk out like a puppy with its tail between its legs!" When it came time for our appearance, no Aide-de-Camp Orr, in spite of numerous calls from those officiating. The girls were almost in tears. With great generosity, one of the other choir's accompanist agreed to play for us. After all that, no one was more surprised than we when the Harford School Choir came in with first place. Celebration continued not only that evening, but after we returned to Moyamba. Just to prove it wasn't a mistake, they did it for several more years!

In 1963, when a special music group was visiting Sierra Leone and giving a few concerts in Freetown, the Choir was invited to visit, so choir members and a few staff drove down for the event. It was exciting to be a part of the audience that night as we waited for the music to begin. There seemed to be some delay in the concert. It wasn't until the United States representative to Sierra Leone came to talk to us that we knew why. With his hands on our shoulders he leaned over to say, with disbelief still in his voice, "President Kennedy has been shot!" Shortly after, they made a public announcement, that in deference, the concert was being cancelled. President Kennedy had been extremely popular in Sierra Leone because of aid his administration had offered the country. A somber Harford School group drove back to the school the next day.

"I Remember" – a lot more, but it will wait for another time!

Elaine Gasser
Home Missionary Red Bird Mission 1950-1953
Missionary to Sierra Leone 1954-1964
Staff Women's Division EUB 1965-1968
United Methodist 1968-1990
(Evangelical United Brethren, United Methodist Church)
(Submitted 2004)

Homecoming at Alexander Chapel

Cherished memories are of those when my family met with a multitude of relatives and friends at the site of the historically oldest Methodist Church in Brazos County in Texas for Homecoming on the fourth Sunday in September each year. The location provided an ideal place for this event, which was always looked forward to with eagerness. The church itself is a simple yet attractive white frame building nestled in a grove of ancient trees. Fastened between some of the tree trunks are wide wooden planks to form picnic tables. A part of the scene is the well-kept rural cemetery separated by a fence of iron. Here the mortal remains of numerous relatives and friends lie. It seemed as if they too shared the happy event with us.

Everyone from the youngest to the oldest shared in the preparation and the event itself. Building and grounds received an extra special cleaning. In each household, hours were spent in preparing delicious foods. The idea of the so-called "potluck" with each family bringing one dish only was not even considered. There would be a variety of salads with potato being the favorite, it seemed. Meats such as fried chicken, roast beef, meatloaf, etc., vegetables, cookies, pies and cakes, with iced tea to drink and perhaps milk or a fruit drink for the children.

Those of us who came early arranged to come early enough to attend Sunday School. Frequently a minister who had served the church in former years was invited to return to preach the Homecoming Service. Sometimes visiting musicians were invited, but for the most part the church choir furnished the music.

After the inspirational service we left the church to meet for what we called "dinner on the ground." Table cloths were spread on the "tables between tree trunks." The food was placed on these. Everyone enjoyed a grand meal and good fellowship.

Ruth Kern
Deaconess USA 1948-1974
(The Methodist Church, United Methodist Church)
(Submitted 2005)

Learning English

I remember writing home after I had worked a few weeks in Rangoon, Burma, and saying, "Hey, Mom, I'm learning a new language–it's called English!

My assignment was to teach music at the Methodist English High School, which was a British English school. Since my term was for only three years, I was not dependent on learning any Burmese (although I did try to learn some).

The principal of the school where I taught was British, and quite insistent that her Burmese students learn <u>proper</u> English.

One day when my choir was learning the Easter hymn, "Were You There When They Crucified My Lord?" the students pronounced the word "were" so that it rhymed with "there" or "wear." I corrected them, saying it should be pronounced to rhyme with "sure."

Before the day was over, I was called into the principal's office and informed that their pronunciation had been correct, and I should not pollute the King's English with my Americanisms.

So from then on I made a real effort to speak correctly. Actually, I learned very fast, and soon any new friends were quite certain I was from England, not the United States.

When I returned home after three years I had developed a really British brogue. Of course, it didn't last after I had been home a while. But I notice I can "turn it on" when I want to.

Jeanne Wintringham
Missionary Burma – –1955 -1958
Sue Bennett College 1968-1992
Commissioned a Deaconess 1977
(The Methodist Church, United Methodist Church)
(Submitted 2005)

Always a Nurse

As I was growing up in West Virginia, I never had the need to decide what work I would be doing and where I would do it. It would be nursing at Red Bird Hospital in SE Kentucky. Not long before I was to graduate from St. Mary's School of Nursing in Huntington, West Virginia, my pastor of the Evangelical United Brethren Church came to me with a question. Although he knew I would soon be on my way to Red Bird, he said he had been told there was an urgent need for nurses in our mission hospital in Española, New Mexico. He wondered whether I would consider going there. I said "yes," as if I had never known about Red Bird Hospital. I was at Española Hospital for a little more than twenty years.

When I arrived there the first of November 1959, it didn't take long to see infants die. Too many of them were taken to the doctor with severe dysentery, pneumonia, etc., late in their illness. But during the first several years I was there we saw changes, due to parents being educated to take the children for medical care before their illness became critical.

One child I will never forget was a four-year-old boy. He and his mother were walking down the pediatric hall for admission. He was wearing a suit, white shirt and tie, and looked as if he might be going to church. We took him to a room, put him to bed, and took his temperature. The first reading of that mercury thermometer made us think it was defective. We took the temperature with two more thermometers, and they had the same reading. The thermometers we had numbered up to 109 and his temperature went beyond that. We got his temperature down, treated his infection, and he went home within a few days.

I found being in New Mexico and working in the Española Hospital for all those years a wonderful experience. In 1980 I went to Red Bird Hospital, the place I had known I was going, but twenty years late!

Margaret Craven
Home Missionary 1959-2003
(Evangelical United Brethren Church, United Methodist Church)
(Submitted 2005)

It Happened in Nasik

It happened in Nasik. Nasik, Western India's Hindu pilgrimage city to which thousands of pilgrims come each year to bathe in the river Godavari, to worship, to seek cleansing and to find solace. Nasik, a city with a three-thousand-year history and dozens of Hindu shrines.

It happened on a Sunday afternoon when I was in my room writing letters. The campus of our *Kristya Lekhan Sanstha*, the Christian Writing Center, was still and empty as our graduate students from all over India had completed their course and gone home. As I wrote I heard footsteps on the steps of our bungalow and went out to see who was there. Before me stood an elderly Hindu gentleman dressed in immaculate white who greeted me with the words, "I saw the sign *Christya Lekhan Sanstha* and I would like to know more about your Jesus."

As we sat and talked in the sitting room he used good English and said something I shall never forget–"I am weary of my Hinduism. Tell me about your Jesus." Weary of his Hinduism! Knowing that the best way for him to learn of Jesus was the Scripture, I asked if I might read him a portion of our Christian Holy Scriptures. He said "yes," so I decided to read him part of St. John's Gospel from Phillips' translation.

Never, before or since, have I seen someone listen to the Word of God with such intense concentration. As I began to read he folded his hands, closed his eyes and bowed his head in worship. I read slowly and carefully, quietly asking God to speak to this devout Hindu. When I finished reading he opened his eyes and asked a very strange question. He asked if I would give him water and something to eat. This I did gladly. He saw my bewilderment and explained that he believed he would be blessed if he had something to eat and drink in the presence of something holy – the Scriptures.

Before he left, I asked if he would like to have the New Testament from which I had read. He was pleased to take it. Since then I have wondered how many thousands of other Hindus are "Weary of their Hinduism."

Ethel Raddon
Missionary with BMMF (an international and interdenominational
missionary fellowship, London)
India 1955-1971
(British Methodist)
(Submitted 2005)

The Last Convoy

My unit was moved from the United States to France in 1945 to provide office support to American troops. I had been a WAC for about two years, and as a staff sergeant I was to supervise and assist in the transition to local civilian control in the PX. Our convoy was made up of about ten ships, all troop ships. Everything was censored and "hush hush," which produced many rumors. Our troopship left Norfolk; and we were told, after we were underway, that we were headed to Le Havre. After we had climbed up the gangplank, we boarded and were assigned to bunks and lockers. The women were assigned to a large room, and we stowed our gear. Our adventure had begun.

Out on that ocean, I had plenty of time to read. The food was army rations, good and plentiful, cooked in a mess on the ship. We WAC's were a very small part of the total personnel aboard, and we certainly couldn't keep up with the men in eating.

The Armistice was signed while we were on our way. We had been hoping, more than expecting, that it would come soon, because the war was winding down. There was a feeling of relief and celebration, but we knew they would not turn the convoy around and take us back home because we were still needed. The civilian structures had been wiped out by the Germans, and it was our job to get things going again and turn it over to the French.

Margaret Overby
Deaconess USA 1963-1983)
(The Methodist Church, United Methodist Church)

Tin Trunk Libraries

"Why should I learn to read? We have a village reader. He reads the letters my son writes to me."

The literacy teachers have their challenges! But there is another challenge down the road. "Where are books in my language?" villagers asked repeatedly. This was the challenge that we in The Commission on Christian Literature faced in the late 50's.

India has fourteen major languages. The Methodist Church works in at least half that number besides several dialects. At that time only 23% of India was literate. Bishop Badley in the 1940's and Bishop Rockey in the 1950's recognized the urgent need for literature in villages.

The Woman's Division through Lucile Colony gave a grant to the Commission on Christian Literature in India. We were thrilled to be able to do something to meet this obvious need. We were finding literature editors in every conference. At that time we had working editors in Bengal, South India; Maharashtra (West India), Gujerat (West India) and Hindi areas.

We began to plan. To each of our eleven conferences we would give fifty Tin Trunk Libraries. In conferences without full-time editors we found volunteers. A member of our staff gave full-time to helping these designated people to select one hundred titles in the vernacular to put into each Tin Trunk.

In each conference ten villages were selected. Each village appointed a village librarian. These librarians met together for a day's training in order to guarantee the books could be issued and accounted for library-style.

Let me share what happened in South India in a Kanarese village. The entire village had become Christian but were originally outcastes. Still, they worked for their Hindi land owners whose larger village was nearby. The Christians had a one-room building where they held Sunday Services and children attended weekday school. During the week their parents worked in the field from dawn to dusk. Free time was limited. But at night they gathered in their one room to read their library books.

The Hindus observed that darkness cut short their reading time, but they also saw the books written in their language! One day a Hindu asked whether they could share the books if they would bring a petromax lamp to make it possible to read after dark. The Christians agreed. This library became the meeting place for Christians and Hindus in an outcast village.

A miracle had happened!

Eunice H. Sluyter
Missionary India
Isabella Thoburn College 5 years
Publisher Lucknow Publishing House 5 years
Treasurer for the Woman's Division
(Dates not given)
(Reformed Church, The Methodist Church)
(Submitted 2005)

Holidays in Small Membership Churches

Some of the most memorable times in working in small membership churches and communities happened around the holidays of Thanksgiving and Christmas in the Odanah Methodist Church. The tradition of Thanksgiving was having a meal, prepared by the women and all the families of the church coming together for a special meal of wild rice, venison, turkey and all the trimmings. We had a short service to thank God for all his blessings of the past year, using grains of corn or some other meaningful item. The lonely in the community were also our guests.

We went into the Advent season with the joy of gathering cedar to make long garlands or wreaths. All the windows and the altar were decorated. Just writing about it, I can almost smell the refreshing odor of cedar and rejoice in celebrating Christmas in a very special way.

December 6 is the celebration of St. Lucia and was celebrated in New York and Wisconsin where we had large Scandinavian communities. On December 6 St. Lucia would be crowned in a ceremony in a church or hotel, and she became the ambassador of good will

124

and love to hospitals, nursing homes and community events. She took gifts to everyone. I used the tradition in Stratford Hollow, New Hampshire.

The final event of the season is Epiphany, the celebration of the coming of the three wise men on January 6. The Episcopal Church would have the beautiful Service of Light. It was to remind us as Christians to take the light of Christ into the world, as the early disciples did.

The generous nature of the people called Native American was something for me to behold. In the spirit of Christ, they many times gave the last cent they had when they knew some-one was in need. We learn from the people with whom we work. It is a mutual sharing.

As Peggy Billings said in a speech she made in Minnesota, "You do not go out to be a success, but to live a life."

It is the seeming little things in life that can say far more than spectacular witnesses to our faith.

Grace Estel
Commissioned Deaconess 1957
(The Methodist Church, United Methodist Church)
(Submitted 2006)

My First Trip to India

I remember when as a young mother of three boys, Mark, age three, John age two, and Paul, three months old, we–Rev. Hackney and I–boarded the *Queen Mary* on a cold winter's morning in March and started our journey to India by way of London. We stayed for one week in England, and then boarded a smaller ship and sailed through the Suez Canal. We stopped in Egypt and Karachi and arrived in Bombay the last part of April. It was very hot and humid.

I remember experiencing the fear of food, water, and strange people with whom we could not communicate, not even being able to understand the broken English. I also remember the dirty sheets on beds in the hotel, and bed bugs too!

After arriving in Delhi and being greeted by a missionary family, I felt secure and not afraid of food and water, and slept for the first time under a mosquito net. We were given a huge upstairs bedroom with a crude bathroom, and a servant brought us buckets of hot water for bathing.

We were going to a village for work where missionaries had not lived before, so there was no mission station in which to stay. It was awesome arriving in India and not having a place to live, and feeling like Jesus who had no place to lay his head.

It was so lovely, however, to go to the Hills soon, where it was cool, and rent a small house for the time we were in language school learning Hindi. This house had mud floors and a mud stove on which to do our cooking. We slowly adjusted to buying food–meat, bread, milk, fruit and vegetables–every day as men came to the house with these supplies. We had employed a cook, and his wife to take care of the children.

I well remember the first convert, a high caste Hindu who came to know the Lord after taking the Gospel of John and reading it.

In the first term of five years we purchased land, built a house, and purchased a jeep to travel the one hundred-mile length of Patiola District. During the five years I worked in education with six small schools where the Bible Women were the teachers. Also at every school I had a preventative health and a food program.

In April before our furlough in May 1964 we dedicated a new church and a parsonage. The people had prayed for this for thirty-seven years.

Yes, there were some health problems with the children, but they all survived and graduated from high school in India, then came to the U.S. for college degrees. All are living and doing well, ranging in age from 44-50. Praise the Lord!

Faye Hackney-Lance
Missionary India 1959-1981
(Married Bishop Lance in India 1997)
(The Methodist Church, United Methodist Church)
(Submitted 2006)

Memories of My Work as a Deaconess

I remember when I struggled with the conviction that God was calling me to a lifetime of service to Christ through the church as a Deaconess–

Little did I know or imagine the rich life in store for me. I remember the bright-eyed little Afro-American girls at Boylan-Haven School in Jacksonville, Florida, during very stressful times off-campus, but rich on-campus experiences with boarding and day students, who in later years have become significant leaders. One is a college president, others teachers, social workers, artists, church, family and community leaders.

I remember the children, youth, mothers and Golden Agers at Centenary Methodist Community Center in Nashville, Tennessee, who had an often drab and impoverished existence, who got great joy from very simple things–an occasional meal, a marshmallow roast, a day or overnight camping experience or club with opportunities to develop leadership skills.

I remember anxious times working with courageous persons on the Mississippi Gulf Coast as Moore Community House in Biloxi became inclusive in its services.

I remember days and late nights writing proposals and much tedium helping to bring matching Federal funds into the state of Mississippi for early childhood/development services, and the joy of seeing children and families develop their God-given potential, physically, mentally, spiritually and socially.

I remember volunteering, after retirement, many nights at United Methodist Seashore Mission, feeding and ministering to wonderful homeless persons, giving hope and encouragement to many for whom life had left little hope for a future. (I was told that I reminded them of their grandmothers.)

I am forever grateful for the wonderfully rich life of priceless memories which have been mine through joyful obedience to God's call upon my life.

Nola Smee
Deaconess USA 1945-1984
(The Methodist Church, United Methodist Church)
(Submitted 2006)

Asheville in 1948

Asheville in August of 1948 was quite different from Asheville today. When I stepped off the train at the old depot, I encountered for the first time the segregated South– the separate drinking fountains, the separate waiting rooms. At Allen high School that first noon I encountered a meal of foods unknown to my northern, Midwest upbringing–black-eyed peas, okra and rice. Warmly welcomed at the school, I knew immediately that God had called me to that place. As teachers in a Black boarding school, we were required to accompany the students to church, shopping, to movies–all of which made us keenly aware that segregation was the way of life in Asheville and the South. With the exception of Warren Wilson College, our basketball team played only other Black high schools. Some of our students were officers in the state student council organization for Black schools. The honor society for Black schools was Crown and Scepter, not the National Honor Society.

Life in a segregated society did not deny the students in our school a quality education in English, mathematics, history, science and other subjects. In addition, emphasis was placed on spiritual growth. Each year every student was enrolled in a Bible class. Chapel attendance was required, as was attendance at Sunday School, Sunday morning worship, and Wednesday evening vespers. All seniors planned and led a chapel service as a requirement for graduation.

In spite of the pattern of segregation in all aspects of society, Women's Societies of Christian Service, Methodist Churches, and organizations such as the YWCA in Asheville and the surrounding area were building bridges of reconciliation. As changes in American society emerged in the fifties and sixties, they had already taken a first step and were ready to move forward.

Ruth Walther
Deaconess USA 1963-1989
Allen High School—1948-1974
Asheville City Schools—1974-1976
St. Paul UM School, Tampa, Fla 1976-1989
(The Methodist Church, United Methodist Church)
(Submitted 2006)

My First Arrival in Singapore

The year 1962 ended in an unforgettable way. I suppose every overseas missionary has a sharp remembrance of arriving in their new country. It was December 31, our little Martha Emily's fourth birthday. She had celebrated at breakfast that morning in Hong Kong, and then again that same night at dinner in Singapore in the home of Esther and Olin Stockwell. That made eight candles---what a special birthday she had! At last, we were in our new home at Trinity Theological College.

Then, the next day, we went to the beach with several families who lived on the Trinity campus. That was quite different from our celebration of New Year's Day in cold New England where we had been living. Since there were so many missionaries from eleven countries and four church denominations, it was easy to adjust to a beautiful new city and a friendly college community.

After nine months of language study I was eager to find a church where I could worship in my new language, Mandarin Chinese. All the churches worshiped in their own dialects, and many had pastors who had been trained in China. Together, the people and their pastors had emigrated and settled all over Southeast Asia, and had established churches in their new communities. They cared for the sojourners from "home," who sometimes stayed in the church when they first arrived. Of all the Methodist Churches, only the Foochow Church had a Mandarin service, which was at 9:00, before the main Foochow service at 11:00. So that is where we went.

From the start I wanted to relate to the congregation, so began to teach the fifth and sixth grade Sunday School class. Fortunately, Bishop Amstutz approved, and when the church started a kindergarten I was asked to be its principal. The kindergarten had a bumpy start. The church officials had not consulted with the government Ministry of Education to get the proper permits and follow regulations. I learned about this when their representative, Miss Ma, came to visit. However, we were able to work together and meet all the requirements. Miss Ma organized kindergarten training workshops and I was invited to help with these. It was wonderful to work with her and to meet the kindergarten teachers from all over the city. These preschools still to this day are privately run and most are in churches.

The children in our kindergarten were from Chinese, Indian, and Malay homes. They were preparing to enter schools where instruction would be in either English or Mandarin--in most cases not the language spoken in their homes. Later I was told that the Foochow Church had started the first bilingual kindergarten to be licensed in Singapore.

But best of all, I had found my way into a church which was in mission in their neighborhood. From Foochow, China, where the Methodist work had been planted, the Foochow Church in Singapore was blooming. And I was a part of it!

Carol Wingeier

Missionary Singapore 1961- 1968

(Volunteer work in many countries)

(The Methodist Church, United Methodist Church)

(Submitted 2006)

God Is Not Partial

Rev. Simon Chisolo was pastor of the Sandoa mission station. He had worked with the early missionaries deciding how to write his language in the English alphabet; then he helped in translating the Scriptures. He was one of the first to be ordained a minister in the Congo Methodist Church. Now, he was to help these new missionaries learn to speak his language.

The school students planted gardens for their food. Rev. Chisolo and I, along with teacher Andre Kasuka, were checking the student gardens when an airliner flew over, a DC4. Rev. Chisolo pointed up and said, "Just look! God gave intelligence to the white people, and left us out here in the dark."

I had to think a bit. Then I said, "Pastor Chisolo, I take exception to that. God is not partial in giving out intelligence."

We thought about the time of Jesus. People were traveling, trading ideas and commerce between countries. The apostle Paul traveled the Mediterranean Sea, taking the witness of the gospel to other people. It was a long, long time until oceangoing ships could sail to the coasts of Africa. Then there were mountains inland from the east and the west coasts. Explorers and missionaries died of unknown diseases. Not until these diseases were identified and medical science learned to prevent and cure them could people from other countries live in these conditions. From a historical perspective the people of Congo have, in a very brief and intense period of time shared culture and commerce with other countries and taken their place in the industrial world.

Now, in 2007, Congo has its commercial airline. Each of the three episcopal areas of the United Methodist Church has its Congolese United Methodist pilot, trained in the United States, flying the aviation services.

Yes, God is not partial.

Everett Woodcock
Missionary Congo 1945-1987
(The Methodist Church, United Methodist Church)
(Submitted 2007)

"It's Because of Mama Woodcock–"

This the Chief said as we enjoyed dinner in his house. The story began long before and this was one of my happy experiences. We first knew him as a young man working with his father in the family general store. This was a progressive family of royal heritage. The time would come that the *Aruund* people would choose this David to be their Paramount Chief, about a half mile from the Kapanga mission station.

While we served a five-year term at Kapanga I asked a neighbor, Suzanne Mbey, if she would like to help me in the kitchen. Most women had full-time responsibility feeding and caring for their families, but Suzanne and her husband had no children. She said she would ask her husband, a chauffeur at the government post. He said, "A good idea." One day I found Suzanne, in the kitchen, writing in a notebook. In my curiosity I asked, "What are you writing?"

"The women in the village ask, 'what do you cook in the missionary house?' So, I try to remember so I can tell them."

We went on furlough and to other appointments, replaced by another couple. They established a school for women in the capital village, and engaged Suzanne Mbey to teach cooking.

Some years later we had opportunity to visit Kapanga. Chief Mwant Yav had invited the missionaries for a special meal at his house, and he had a display of sumptuous food. He thanked everyone for accepting his invitation and then said, "It is because of Mama Woodcock; she taught Mama Suzanne in her kitchen, then Mama Suzanne taught the women of our village, and prepared this meal this evening."

Bishop Shungu sometimes said, "The happiness of the mother is to see her family enjoy her food."

This was one of my happy days.

Vera Woodcock
Missionary Congo 1945-1987
(The Methodist Church, United Methodist Church)
(Submitted 2007)

Friday, March 27, 1964–5:45 P.M

5:30 p.m.–Six girls sitting around the supper table at Jesse Lee Home in Seward, Alaska (now the Alaska Children's Services in Anchorage) were being served creamed chicken.

Suddenly, a loud rumble! It was an old building–my first thought was that the old boiler was boiling up and we'd all be gone!

Sam, a house parent with his wife, Shirley for the boys' group, stood up and commanded, "Everybody out!"

We all obeyed the command and went to the old school bus, used to take children to church. There was one step on the way outside, and Roxanne lost one shoe, but we kept going.

As we waited for the bus, I asked why we didn't head up the highway to Anchorage. The answer came back–the highway was impassable, and the oil tanks on the Bay were on fire.

I later learned that my father had seen on the eleven o'clock news in Western Pennsylvania that Seward had been wiped off the map by an earthquake.

The bus took us to a four-room school building, no longer used, while they returned to Jesse Lee's kitchen to get all the sandwich meat, milk, etc. , as we had not eaten supper.

We were then taken to a building used by Air Force personnel for recreation. Shortly after we got all the children bedded down, we were told to get everyone up, because of the threat of a tidal wave.

On Saturday there were aftershocks. We were taken to the local high school in downtown Seward to eat.

Sunday morning we were told we could write a note to our families, and they would fly it out to the "Lower 48." I still have that scrap of paper sent to my parents.

After several days' discussion we were allowed back into our buildings, but before many days were told to pack up–we were moving to the Boys' building. Our section had been damaged and would be torn down.

Then after some time a new Administrator arrived and a new building was built near Anchorage, closer to the Alaska Native Hospital.

Words cannot describe the move to the new facilities. There were cottages–one for girls–and television (one channel)–a separate apartment for the House Parent–an office for a

Counselor–everything brand new. The main meal was prepared in the Administrative Building and delivered to the cottage to be served.

I have always said I was not sorry to have lived through an earthquake, but I do not wish to do it again!

Jean Morgan
US2 1952-1954
Deaconess USA 1956-1992
(The Methodist Church, United Methodist Church)
(Submitted 2007)

A Crowded Subway Ride

I looked at my watch and realized that rush hour had started in Sao Paulo, Brazil. There I was, still at the Child Center at Jabaquara Methodist Church. I hurried as fast as I could and walked up the hill to the closest subway station, which was also the starting point.

The train was already beginning to get crowded. Standing, I held on to the handle device close to the door, thinking that surely I could get off o.k. when I reached Liberdade Station.

At each stop more and more passengers got on. As we approached Liberdade I could hardly move, and I had to maneuver with my elbows to get closer to the door. When we arrived at Liberdade Station, I and a few others were trying desperately to get off, while a crowd was pushing and shoving their way in.

I did manage to land safely and whole, but minus one shoe. While I was panicky, wondering how I was going to get to my apartment two blocks away, just as the door was closing, my shoe came flying out. I did have time to yell *obrigada*–thank you–before the train moved on.

Sarah Frances Bowden
Born in Brazil of Methodist missionary parents
Brazil Contract Worker, Woman's Division
1947-1950
Commissioned a Missionary 1950
Brazil 1952-1992
(The Methodist Church, United Methodist Church)
(Submitted 2008)

135

An Effective Ending to a Worship Service

After graduating from Scarritt College, I was employed as a Director of Christian Education at St. Luke's Methodist Church in Jackson, Mississippi. On a Sunday afternoon the Senior High MYF decided to go for a picnic supper and worship service on the Natchez Trace. In the quietness of the worship service a friendly cow came up to the fence separating her pasture from our picnic spot. She looked the group over and then gave a hearty "moo."

Immediately one of the boys, in the same tone and pitch, returned her moo. That "moo" was as effective in ending the worship service as an "Amen" would have been.

Susan Carmichael
Deaconess USA Commissioned 1960
(The Methodist Church, United Methodist Church)
(Submitted 2008)

Adventures in Foreign Lands

There were three of us girls, recent college graduates, ready to tackle the world and as green as grass. We sailed from New York to Liverpool, England, on our way to Burma to serve three years as short-term missionaries. There would be several days' layover before getting on the next ship that would take us to Burma. We decided to spend them in London rather than the less exciting Liverpool.

We succeeded in getting on the right train to London, and found an inexpensive hotel. Since there was no bathroom in any of our rooms, we started walking down the hall in search of one.

All the doors looked alike except one with the letters "W C" We surmised that perhaps that was a room reserved for Winston Churchill, and kept walking.

Finally, we summoned the courage to try that door, since there was no other possibility. Just as we approached the door, a man walked out of it. We kept walking.

It took a trip down to the lobby to learn that "W C" stood for Water Closet, and was used by both men and women.

****

The American Embassy often invited the Americans working in Rangoon, Burma to attend special programs and receptions. Such was the case when Marion Anderson came and sang in Rangoon while I was teaching music at the Methodist High School.

At the reception following her concert, I was able to introduce myself to her . . . Without a moment's hesitation, she responded, "Oh, then we have three things in common; we are both Americans, we are both musicians, and we are both Christians."

The obvious difference–the color of our skin–was so unimportant. She had quickly spotted the important things.

Jeanne Wintringham
Missionary Burma – –1955 -1958
Sue Bennett College 1968-1992
Commissioned a Deaconess 1977
(The Methodist Church, United Methodist Church)
(Submitted 2008)

Anticipating Brooks-Howell as "Home"

"Who would <u>choose</u> to live in a Retirement Home?" questioned more than one of our 1957 US- 2 group, as we toured the Asheville facility the second summer after its first residents had moved in. (My memory may be faulty at this point, but I believe the visitation took place when the US-2's of 1956 and 1957 came together for an evaluation of their training – the summer of 1958.)

My recollection is that I knew at least one of the residents at that time, Mary Kesler, a retired missionary from the Kansas West Conference, who felt I was being called to be a deaconess. When I found her in a room at Brooks-Howell, she was confined to a total care unit, having suffered a life-after-death experience. Her description to me of that event was typical – a figure enshrouded in light, a firm grip on her elbow, a loving voice asking her what her wish was as to the direction they were moving, and her answer, "As You will, Lord." Suddenly she was back in Brooks-Howell Home, without a clue as to what she was still expected to accomplish. My understanding is that she was bedfast for the remainder of her years there, perhaps at least three. Who knows if that conversation with me was all the Lord required of her?!

Nothing about the facility itself lingers in my memory. Mary's very limited energy was focused on encouraging me to continue on the path toward using my teaching skills in a church-related vocation. Knowing my family background rather well, she even pointed out the benefits that Brooks-Howell would offer me in thirty-eight years! She attributed her being able to visit with me that day to the caring community and action-oriented skills surrounding her when her body collapsed in her bathroom some weeks preceding our conversation. Thus the seed was planted that one day I would be at home on 29 Spears Avenue in Asheville, North Carolina.

Somehow the next twenty-five or so years went by without my future coming to the forefront, until an invitation came from the Deaconess Program Office to participate in a pre-retirement event happening in early August 1985 or 1986 at Lake Junaluska. One of our tours brought us to Brooks-Howell. The address was still 29 Spears Avenue, but for the life of me, I do not remember having seen the building before, or having entered it from the street that day or any earlier day. The only vignette in my mind is a big dining room with a series of round tables seating seven or eight residents, with sporadic empty places for members of our group to be seated. Our group's plates were brought to us, but the able-bodied diners at each table went to a central serving area to pick up their filled plates.

138

Who were the residents then? The only one I am somewhat confident of having talked to was Linda Frost, because I was so surprised that someone younger than I had already been welcomed "Home." Another new learning on that visit was the existence of apartments outside the main building. My hostess in her apartment was someone familiar to me, but neither she nor the ambience of her life style remain imprinted in my foggy memory. The final days of the seminar concentrated on making our retirement days financially secure, and getting into Brooks-Howell was my point of focus.

"Fast Forward" to the first of November 2005. A year had gone by since the death of a cherished friend, who had been responsible for my coming to Jackson, Mississippi thirty years earlier to share her house. The retirement facility where I lived announced the monthly rent for the next year would be $30 higher than that of the previous year. I had already begun to question my ability to manage the situation financially. Now I had only until the 5th of the month to let management know if I would be renewing my lease. Presto! A phone call to Brooks-Howell, where I had mailed an application at the end of the summer (although sent to the Deaconess Program Office in New York), brought the reply the next day: "Come on up! Just let us know the details of your arrival. We'll work out your permanent living arrangements when you get here!" That night I went to sleep with this tune floating in my head: "I'll be home for Christmas!"

Rosemary Scheuerman
US 2   1957-1959
Deaconess USA 1961-1991
(The Methodist Church, United Methodist Church)
(Submitted 2008)

A Journey in Sarawak

I remember our journey up the Rejang River in Sarawak, where I first met Lorraine Gribbens. It was 1965 and Doug, our daughter Ruth, and I went to Sarawak to visit the missionaries who were working there.

First we visited the seminary in Sibu. The students were taught in three languages--English, Chinese, and Iban. There we visited Jim and Charlotte Hipkins, old seminary friends who were teaching there. On campus we met people who in later years became good friends. The Chinese church in Sarawak has just this year celebrated their 100th anniversary.

Next we continued our journey up the Rejang River on the legendary "launch." It was a bit like a houseboat--a wooden barge with a few rooms where passengers could sleep. Out on deck were many passengers with their livestock, produce, and supplies to sell or use for the next few months.

The next morning we arrived in Kapit and visited Christ Hospital. This hospital was founded by Dr. Harold Brewster, who by then was working at the Mission Board in New York as the doctor for all missionaries. It was he who decided if we were physically ready to be sent out, and examined us when we returned.

The hospital was in a remote village in a Borneo rainforest where there were no roads. There was only one doctor to attend to all who came for help - Lorrie Crisologo. His wife Dorothy was the anestheologist, and Lorraine Gribbens was the pharmacist. I love you, Lorraine, and remember the interesting journey upriver to see the place where you worked and served.

(Lorrain Gribbins and Jim Hipkins were/are residents at Brooks-Howell Home. The Crisologos were/are residents at a UMC retirement center in Asheville.)

Missionary Singapore 1963- 1970

Volunteer in several other countries

(The Methodist Church , United Methodist Church

(Submitted 2008)

The Day Leonardo Came Back to Church

I remember the day Leonardo came back to church. It was a victory of sorts. He and his family were active members of the Arroyito Methodist Church. He was a librarian at the Methodist School in town, the school where I served when I first went to Argentina. After the national church ordained me, I had served in several churches. No one, to my knowledge, had questioned my role as a "woman pastor." Then I was appointed to Arroyito and warmly received by everyone except Leonardo.

He came to church regularly for a few weeks and then dropped out. I asked his wife and his mother about his absence, but both gave vague answers and seemed to be embarrassed by the question. Suspecting that I might be the problem, I talked to two strong lay leaders, both of whom were good friends of Leonardo. They confirmed my suspicions and suggested that I let them talk to him. They did and then reported that he had told them that he had nothing against me as a person, that he liked my sermons and the way I did things. He just thought it was wrong for the church to appoint a woman as pastor. One of the men said that he had carefully read through the New Testament, finding nothing to justify the position held by Leonardo.

Months passed, and Leonardo's mother became ill. It was a long illness with much suffering, and a final release in death. Through the months of agony I visited her regularly and presided at the funeral. Leonardo thanked me and told me that he knew how much my visits and prayers had meant to his mother. Soon after, he appeared in church. That was where he belonged in a time of mourning–even with a <u>woman</u> pastor. It seems that he had been influenced by a son-in-law who belonged to a very conservative church, but when the chips were down he joined his wife and daughter back at Arroyito. I thanked the Lord for bringing him back.

Patricia (Pat) Richardson
Missionary Argentina
(Woman's Society of Christian Service)
1954-1997
(The Methodist Church, United Methodist Church)
(Submitted 2008)

Christmas at Wesley House

The season [December] causes me to remember Christmas time at Wesley Community House in Louisville, Kentucky. Getting ready always meant a trip to our Camp Merry Ledges to get a tree that would fit in the lobby only if we cut off the top and removed two ceiling tiles! One time one of the Day Care parents looked at it and backed out the door to see where it came out of the roof! The top became the lovely tree that was placed in the large living room/game room/meeting room. Various in-house groups decorated "the Wesley" annually with a theme such as Christmas stories, Around the World, carols and songs, symbols of Christmas, etc. It was like entering and serving in a fairyland.

We were instrumental in calling the neighborhood churches together to coordinate programs and services. Christmas was a great opportunity to showcase all of us. Wesley House took leadership in planning and executing a progressive dinner and tour that included all the churches, Wesley House and the house in which Thomas Edison once lived. (Wesley had been able to restore it as a museum with a tearoom–a popular fund raiser for us.)

Family Dinner with 150-200 people of all ages with Santa Claus and St. Paul UMC puppets was always special. The picture is a candid shot of the children spontaneously kneeling at the nativity displayed in the case in the lobby

Another special remembrance is of the Wesley Wearhouse, a thrift shop operated solely by volunteers. When I left WCH in 1988 the Wearhouse was taking in $40,000 a year, owning and maintaining its own building. That's another story!

June Fischer
USA 2 1960-1962
Commissioned Deaconess 1963
(The Methodist Church, United Methodist Church)
(Submitted 2009)

A Transformation

Carol and I served in Singapore eight years in the 1960s, where I taught at Trinity Theological College--in both English and Mandarin Chinese. During our first term my Chinese was still rather shaky, so I tended to associate more with English-speaking persons and congregations. Some of these were merchants who were benefitting from trade with Americans associated with the war in Vietnam, and were thus supportive of my country "holding the line against Communism." I remember one Thanksgiving writing a letter to friends at home expressing gratitude for the U.S. stand in Southeast Asia.

However, during our second term, as my Chinese improved, I had more and more opportunity to know Chinese-speaking people, who tended to be working-class, and began to hear their perspective on the war.

As director of field education I often visited the students in their churches to supervise their work. One Sunday I went with a Chinese department student by boat across the Johore Straits to visit his church in a small village in southern Malaya accessible only by sea. After church a farmer family invited us to their home where they asked the student pastor to conduct a service of thanksgiving for his sow which had just given birth to a litter of piglets. Their simple faith, generous hospitality, and profound gratitude to God deeply impressed me.

A couple of weeks later this student came to me with a question from this same farmer: "If yours is a Christian country, why are they over here in Southeast Asia killing our Asian peasants?"

I had no ready answer.

Putting myself in this farmer's position, I could see his puzzlement and the contradiction in my role. I was there in Asia telling people about the love of Jesus, the Prince of Peace, while my nation was there destroying villages like his and killing farmers like him.

This was a profound and deeply disturbing confrontation for me, and forced me to rethink my hitherto mindless support of my country's foreign policy. I began to realize that the U.S. presence there was undermining my efforts to teach that God is love and Jesus saves. This encounter was the beginning of my transformation into becoming a peace and justice activist--a patriot who loves my country enough to criticize it when it's wrong, and a

Christian who tries to put love of God above loyalty to Caesar when the two are in conflict, as they were then and have often been before and since.

Douglas Wingeier
Missionary Singapore 1963- 1970
Faculty, Trinity Theological College, Singapore
Faculty, Garrett-Evangelical Theological Seminary,
Evanston, IL, 1970-97
Short-term volunteer faculty, theological schools in

Samoa, Korea, Malaysia, Indonesia, Philippines,

Cuba, and Bethlehem Bible College in Palestine

(The Methodist Church, United Methodist Church)

(Submitted2009)

God At Work Through Wesley House Centers

I was fortunate to serve on the staff of Wesley House, and I tell my story so that you will know what God brought to pass in that place. You have to realize that any story I tell about what happened there is a story of what Wesley House meant to the neighborhood.

For instance, there was a little boy named Jerome (not his real name, of course), about eight years old, who came often to the playground. He could not participate in playground activities because he could not focus on what he should be doing long enough to be part of the group. He would play about thirty minutes, then he broke down and turned over tables, chairs, playground equipment all over the place. He could not stand being unable to do it all himself, and I had to take him home because he simply could not function on the playground. His mother was an alcoholic, which made life extremely difficult for him.

One day while he was having such a hard time they came to get me to come and take him away from the other children. I brought him to the office and closed the door. He spat on the floor. I told him that was enough of that kind of behavior, and he would need to clean the floor. I got him a bucket and some rags and I got down on the floor and helped him. We got the mess cleared up, and I showed him how to put the bucket away.

Jerome began to change as he grew older and when he ran into "no-no" flags, I tried to help him understand himself and the world he lived in. I saw him learning to think before he acted. He made it to high school, and one day he told me that he wanted to go to college. I had already made arrangements for him to go to a technical school because I felt sure that was the place where he would have the greatest possibility for success. But Jerome was determined to go to college. I felt that he deserved my support in making his own decision.

I talked to the President of Andrew College. I also made a serious commitment to the college to try to help Jerome. I made many trips to bring him home, and on one trip when I had to go get him, I was aware of his anxiety as he asked me why everybody didn't have the same kind of problems he had. I told him that the things that happened to him at home and in other places made it difficult for him to take responsibility for his own actions. We talked more, and he seemed to find some peace.

He came back home and went to Technical School, where the stresses were not so extreme for him and he had more understanding and support. He was nineteen then, and he felt the year at college had helped him. After graduation he got a job in a local store. He told me how pleased he was to be able to make his own money. One morning while we were talking, he said, "Miss A, you understand me better than anybody else." I knew that he had grown up. He had matured enough to work on his problems himself. When our office was moved Jerome continued to come by just to stay in touch.

(As told to Ann Janzen.)

Doris Alexander
Wesley Community Center, Atlanta 1953-1955
Commissioned Deaconess 1957
Wesley Community Center, Atlanta 1957- 1993
10 years as a volunteer in three agencies
(The Methodist Church, United Methodist Church)
(Submitted 2009)

A Senior at Harris

To be a senior at Harris Memorial College was a big deal! A senior preparing to be a deaconess became a member of a gospel team. A team composed of four students would go to a barrio where there was a Methodist Church. There they could practice what they had learned. As a newly-appointed missionary I "inherited" the Gospel Team from Leila Dingle, who was at one time a resident of Brooks-Howell.

Armed with a Bible and sometimes a mosquito net, we set off on a Saturday afternoon in the black Chevrolet. We knew we had reached our destination when children's shouts of welcome pierced the air as the girls piled out of the car. They never mistook the blue skirt and white blouse school uniform!

The first activity was the Sunday School under the big Acacia tree. The children sang heartily the songs they had learned on a previous visit. The Bible story was enhanced by the colorful flannelgraph. By this time many, old and young, had gathered round to see what was happening. The crafts with crayons (thanks to a WSCS circle in the States) was exciting, though knees had to be substituted for desks. Lastly– a new game. What fun! And then, hand in hand, student and child were off to their homes to tell of the coming activities.

Saturday night was Youth Night, with devotions, a lesson and games. The circle game required everyone to hold hands–oh, this was something new! Would the elders approve of this? A pitch was made for attendance at the Christmas Institute. Many future deaconesses first learned of Harris here, and responded to the call to become full-time Christian workers.

Sunday morning activities were the responsibility of the Gospel Team. Demonstration Sunday School classes taught by the team were to inspire the local teachers with new ideas and methods. The team always had a musical number during the worship service and the missionary teacher gave the message.

It was the women's turn on Sunday afternoon. The girls felt less confident in preparing a sample WSCS program. The students expressed their insecurity with "They are older than we are, ma'am, we can't tell them what to do!" But the gracious women made the team feel their new ideas were wonderfully appreciated.

Four o'clock! Time to start back to Manila! What a clamor in the back seat of the Chevrolet, "It was wonderful!" "Did you notice Bill?" "I wish we had a Gospel Team every weekend!"

As we drove into the Harris compound, Dr. Prudencia Fabro, president of Harris Memorial College, stood on the porch to welcome us back with "Glad you're back safely. Did you have a restful weekend?"

"Restful! I worked harder on Gospel Team weekends than any other time of the year!" was my reply. "But it was great, and worth every minute! But most important, the girls are learning what it means to be a deaconess!"

Elizabeth Johannaber
Missionary China 1947-1951
Philippines 1952 -1963
Singapore 1976-1980
(The Methodist Church, Woman's Division, United Methodist Church)
(Submitted 2010)

The Birth and Near Death of Our Youngest Child

Remembering is often an iffy thing. To one it might be this way and to another that way, but this is how I remember the most memorable experience of my past.

We were an excited couple with two small boys getting ready for our first adventure to a place halfway around the world, Indonesia. We had gotten much advice about what we should take of our worldly possessions to this tropical paradise, but we still took far too much in the drums that we shipped, which, by the way, arrived a year after we did. One thing I did take in my suitcase was a Lamaze book for help in natural childbirth. We knew at the time we might want to expand our family and we also knew that medical facilities might be limited.

Two years later I found myself holding onto the cold tile wall trying to make my way to the delivery room. On my insistence Don had taken me to the hospital early on the morning of July 20, 1970, on our Vespa motor scooter. (A neighbor had offered his car when the time came for me to go to the hospital but Don insisted we could easily get there -- I sort of agreed!) We had house guests that were leaving that morning to fly to visit our missionary friends, Warren and Jo Harbert, in Jambi. So, when not so frequent pains started that morning I wanted to get out of the house before anyone got up. Being assured I was in good hands at the hospital, Don went home to take care of our guests and children. When pains soon got harder and frequent calls for the nurse failed to get a response, I just went to the delivery room myself. Twenty minutes later our darling blonde baby boy, Cary Wayne, was born. My Indonesian Chinese doctor was amazed that I didn't yell and carry on like other westerners he had helped in delivery. Little did he know that I didn't have time to do that but also I had religiously studied my Lamaze book. (That was my first "God thing.")

Our pediatrician, Dr. Gepito, was a tall middle aged Javanese doctor who was fluent in English, Dutch, Indonesian, and probably other languages. He told me to be sure not to let the nurses in the hospital give our baby the smallpox immunization. He knew we would get this shot in a year as was recommended. I understood all too well what he was talking about because I had just corrected a thesis for a medical student. The topic was the instances of infant mortality after newborns received the smallpox vaccination. It concluded that there were a high percentage of deaths from this immunization but it was far less than the deaths that occurred if the infant became ill with smallpox. The problem was that parents usually did not take their babies back to the doctor at the recommended time, so the shots were given before they left the hospital. I was really troubled by this position but understood the reasoning. When the nurse brought in our beautiful newborn for the first time, you can imagine my horror when I saw a big bandage on his leg. I asked about it and she casually said, "Oh, that's his smallpox vaccination. All babies get this." I was so angry and upset but really didn't know how to express that anger in Indonesian. (That was the second "God thing.")

We happily went home after a week. Cary was a "spitter," just like his older brother, Steven. It was more than spitting. You would have thought he hadn't kept down a bit of milk. Dr. Spock was my constant reference book for childhood diseases. He called it projectile vomiting. The advice was that if this persists, see your pediatrician. Our first two-week visit did raise some concern because Cary had lost weight. Dr. Gepito said he wanted to watch Cary very carefully but he was going out of town for two weeks. He assured us he would be leaving a very competent resident and he would alert her of her condition. After two days Cary seemed to be worse, so we returned to the doctor. Sure enough, it was almost like she expected us, and immediately sent us to the hospital. She wanted to observe my nursing him and his response.

Now if you haven't been in a hospital in a third world country, it is quite a different experience. In this clean Catholic hospital the rooms were like glass cages running down the middle of two hallways. Families came and camped out in the hallways where they could easily see the patients and respond to their needs. Being the private person that I am, this was not a good scenario. Immediately there was a crowd around our window looking in at this white lady sitting on a mattress on the floor with her very sick baby. The resident seemed to be at a loss as to what to do. First she said maybe he was allergic to my breast milk. Naturally I wanted to try anything, but was a bit fearful of their sterile techniques in preparing the formula. After that seemed to make no difference they said he would need an I.V. Their method was to inject the fluid with a very large needle into his back which bubbled up like a very big balloon. I was so afraid. Then a small still voice said, "Remember I am with you always, even to the ends of the earth." I remembered! A surgeon was called in and said, "I think he is obstructed but we can't operate on babies here. So if you want him to have surgery you will have to go to Singapore."

Don, having sensed that we might have to go out of the country to Singapore, had already started the long process of getting an exit-re-entry permit from the immigration office. They wanted this paper then another one and on it went for several days. Don began to suspect they wanted a bribe but being the new missionaries that we were, we were not willing to pay a bribe. Finally, the officer said, "Well, I can't give you a stamp because the baby doesn't have the smallpox immunization." Oh, but thank God, he did! So we got the permit.

That day there was no direct flight to Singapore so we booked to leave Palembang from the hospital, fly to Jakarta, and then on to Singapore, arriving the same day. The resident again gave Cary an I.V. in the back and told us to be sure to go straight to the hospital because he would need immediate care. When we arrived in Jakarta to get our connecting flight, there were no flights to Singapore that day as we had been told. We were forced to spend the night in a hotel pacing the floor with a sick baby and praying that we would arrive in time for his urgent medical care. Missionary friends, Peter and Susan Purdy, who lived in Jakarta, came and comforted us during that long night.

The next day two distraught parents, two active little boys, and a sick baby arrived at the Singapore Adventist Hospital at the end of the surgeon's office hours. His presence was calming. He immediately showed us how Cary was obstructed and said he would do surgery the next morning. Just like Dr. Spock had written in his book, it was *hypertrophy pyloric stenosis.*

Don and the children enjoyed a week at the New Leone Guest House while Cary and I recovered in the hospital. I admit I was a bit envious of the delicious food they were enjoying at this very British guest house. Then I remembered all the silverware at each place setting and was glad I wasn't there to witness the numerous times Steven and Keith dropped theirs on the floor.

Since my brother is a surgeon, we chose to call him to tell our parents about Cary's surgery. When I heard his voice, of course I began to cry. He said in a very professional voice, "Oh, that's a very common surgery. I did three of those this week. Nothing to it!" If we had been in the same room, I would have thrown something at him. Then I composed myself and said, "Please, just tell Mother and Daddy we're all O.K." (And that was a "God thing.")

Ramona Turman
Missionary Indonesia 1968- 1972, 1992-1995,
1999-2005
Volunteer in Indonesia in 2007-2008
(United Methodist Church)
(Submitted 2010)

The Phone Call

I remember the phone call–out of the blue and completely unexpected: "Virginia, I am Bob Smith*, and I would like to volunteer to help in our church's disaster response."

"Well, that's great. Tell me more."

"I was a policeman in Atlanta for many years, and retired on disability, but I can do home repair. My wife is caring for an elderly mother and cannot be away, but I would like to do this."

We talked for a while, and I got a sense of this person, and finally I said, "There's one place that needs a person just like you. _____ County in West Virginia had a flood some time ago. The United Methodists and Mennonites have had volunteer teams doing the major repair. The person I sent to coordinate the teams and work with families has gone home. This is a very poor area, and there are still hurting families. I have been praying for the right person to send, who can work alone and do this–but I must tell you, this is a remote area and folks are very suspicious of outsiders."

His reply was, "I grew up in that very county in West Virginia."

He worked for several weeks completing the repairs, while he lived in his covered truck in a nearby state park. He was truly an answer to prayer.

The above is but one example of the way God so often seemed to send just the right person or right resources to meet a specific human need during my years as disaster network coordinator for United Methodist Committee on Relief.

My connection to this network began when there was no network, and tornadoes made a path of destruction through Cherokee County , North Carolina, where I was serving as church and Community Worker. My experience there, combined with that of many other folks, created this network from point zero to the really amazing response of many United Methodists to the needs of thousands of hurting folks, each year. It has been an amazing and humbling journey

*Not his real name

Virginia Miller

152

US2—Church and Community Worker 1956-1958
Church and Community Worker—1959-1976
Commissioned Deaconess 1962
UMCOR 1977-1998   (worker and staff)
(The Methodist Church, United Methodist Church)
(Submitted 2010)

The Longest Night

It was the last night of the trip. Two weeks earlier I had boarded the ship with Lois and Elsie in New York City. We stood on the deck and waved at my parents who stood on the dock. It would be five years before I would return to the United States. The three of us were being sent by the Board of Missions of the The Methodist Church to serve as missionaries in South America. Elsie would work in a social center in Rio de Janeiro [Brazil], Lois in Crandon Institute in Montevideo [Uruguay], and I was headed for a school in Rosario, Argentina. There were three of us, and we were going to three different countries along the eastern coast of the Continent.

The trip had been great. We stopped at two islands in the Caribbean for sightseeing and then in Bahia, a Brazilian city known for its 365 Catholic churches. When we sailed into Rio, there was a band on the dock welcoming us with rousing music. Among the many people waiting to receive arriving friends and relatives, we spotted a group from the institution where Elsie would be working. They held large signs so that we could easily see them from the ship. How exciting it was! Lois and I debarked with Elsie and were graciously shown about the city. Then came evening and time to say goodbye to Elsie.

The next stop was Santos, and then we arrived in Montevideo. The ship docked early and we were still in our cabin when half a dozen folks from Crandon appeared at the cabin door to welcome Lois and help her with her hand luggage. They gave us a royal welcome and took us to see the city and the school. Then evening came, and time to say goodbye to Lois. Suddenly I was alone. Well, not really. The ship was still full of people, but not <u>my</u> people. The overnight trip from Montevideo to Buenos Aires was starting, and I felt completely alone.

When the dock was no longer in sight, I headed for the lounge where the remaining passengers were to go through the immigration formalities. Argentine officials had boarded the ship and did they look <u>official</u>. If only Elsie and Lois would have been with me to go through this ordeal—

I hardly slept that night, but lay on my bunk listening to the waves of the River Plate (*el rio de la Plata*) hit against the side of the ship and wondering about the coming day. I had never doubted my decision to go to Argentina for five years until that night when I found myself alone in a cabin meant for three or four.

At daybreak I was up quickly, rushing to the deck, ready to see the land that I would call home and hoping to see someone or if possible, several some ones, there to welcome me.

154

Nobody was in sight except the dock workers, busy securing the ship, letting down the gang planks, and ignoring the passengers hanging over the railings. Oh, and a few sea gulls. Running along the dock was a long grey drab building, something like a warehouse. No band, no people to welcome our boat, none at all.

Finally, the loud speaker announced that passengers could disembark. I picked up my belongings, swallowed an unborn tear, and made my way to the gangplank. On dry land we were herded into the grey building where the larger luggage had been unloaded and was stacked all over the huge area. After wandering, and being accidentally pushed and shoved by others, just as confused as myself, I noticed large signs hanging from the rafters. Each sign was a letter of the alphabet, and it didn't take too long to discover that the luggage was placed in areas according to the name on the label. So I headed to find the R luggage. At this moment a young woman rushed up and said, "Are you Pat Richardson?"

The surprise and relief left me speechless, so I nodded. She turned out to be Helen Safstrom, a missionary who was Director of the school in Rosario. With her was a man, who spoke no English, but who I learned was the President of the Board of Directors of the school. He and his wife had driven Helen the three hundred kilometers from Rosario to Buenos Aires.

Helen explained that no visitors were allowed on the dock. Neither were they permitted in the customs building. She was quite sure that Señor Petit had bribed the guard to get them in.

So I breathed a sigh of relief. The long night was over, and I was no longer alone.

Patricia (Pat) Richardson
Missionary Argentina
(Woman's Society of Christian Service)
1954-1997
(The Methodist Church, United Methodist Church)

(This article was found in Pat's papers after her death, and printed in the May-June 2011 *Serendipitor*.)

Praying for a Pig

From 1966-68 I was a US-2 in south Texas. The church and community assignment was a joint endeavor of the Rio Grande and Southwest Texas conferences. There was one English-speaking church and there were three Spanish/English-speaking churches. For me, going from the mountains of West Virginia to the flat lands of south Texas was an interesting adventure. It was quite a learning experience, living in the midst of two cultures who did not always understand or appreciate one another. I went from a fairly homogeneous culture to a place where there was definitely discrimination based on ancestry, race, language, and culture. I was very much accepted and loved by the people of a culture different from my own.

One of my fondest memories includes working with the Methodist Youth Fellowship in two of the churches. One youth named Eddie was a member of his local 4-H club. He was raising a pig which he intended to show at the local fair. Unfortunately, shortly before the time of the fair, the pig quit eating and began to lose weight. If you have ever raised an animal to show, you know this is a serious situation. Eddie was understandably distressed. One day after our MYF meeting he asked me if I would pray for his pig. It was the first time I had ever had such a request. But I did pray for Eddie's pig, and you know what? The pig began to eat and thrive and went on to win a ribbon at the fair that year. My prayers were coveted for all manner of things for some time after that. It is indeed a fond memory.

By the way, Eddie is the brother of Inelda Gonzalez, our current* Women's Division president.

*At the time of writing

Marilyn S. Benson
U.S. 2 1966-1968
Church and Community Worker 1966-2007
Commissioned Deaconess 1971
(The Methodist Church, United Methodist Church)
(Submitted 2011)

Feeling God's Glory

When reading the *Disciplines* one morning, I read the story of Moses and the burning bush. He felt God's glory as he walked on holy ground.

I certainly felt God's glory as I knelt on a dirt floor in a poor home and took holy communion as it was translated into *Nauhtl*, an Indian language. While talking with Bishop Ruiz of the Methodist Church of Mexico, he had suggested that I visit Huitzlan, a small isolated Indian village in the state of Puebla, to determine the possibility of initiating medical work in that area. What an experience! I knew that God wanted me to serve in that community. This was a remote village, in an extremely rainy section of the country, accessible by vehicle about a third of the year. The rest of the time one entered by foot or horseback (I am not a horseback fan). We had no running water or electricity. Yet I loved it. The clinic grew and since most of the time I was the only medical person in the area, I treated lots of GI, respiratory, and skin problems. If patients were critically ill, they had to be carried out of the mountains to a small hospital. I never mastered the *Nauhtl* language, although I am fluent in Spanish, but managed enough to be able to treat basic problems. I did only one delivery as they had their own local midwives, but learned to treat lots of post partum infections. The clinic/house was completed shortly after I returned from furlough and I found a wonderful Christian lady from Mexico City who was willing to come live with me. During the time we were there the church was completed. I still cannot hear the hymn, "Go tell it on the Mountain," without thinking of that village. After about a year and a half, I realized it was simply too rural for me and after much prayer and discussion with church leaders, I decided to return to the States. Now I look back on it and know that God planned even that. I had only been back a few months when my mother had cancer surgery and after a second surgery she came to live with me. God had brought me back to care for her.

After talking about my medical experiences, I have frequently been asked, "But what were your missionary experiences?" What better way to teach God's love, than to care for his children? Matthew 25 states "I was sick and you came to visit, I was hungry and you fed me. . .." Also, I can look back and see the impact on people's lives. And it continues. God's glory has been evident in all that I do.

Marjorie (Jorie) Ruegger
Missionary Mexico 1 966 -1978
(The Methodist Church, United Methodist Church)
(Submitted 2011)

I Never Wanted to be a Deaconess

I never wanted to be a Deaconess, but God apparently had different plans for my life. During my childhood and youth my family and I were active in our local Methodist Churches in Louisville, Kentucky.

Then the war began, and following graduation from the University of Louisville I entered the WAVES. My mother said, "Betsy, be sure to find a church to attend wherever you are sent."

After the war I entered Scarritt College for Christian Workers in Nashville, Tennessee. Later I went to work for the General Board of Missions of the Methodist Church in New York. There Mary Lou Barnwell, head of the Deaconess Office, began to challenge me to become a Deaconess. That was the beginning of a life that enabled me to become a world traveler.

After some years in New York I was elected Director of the Deaconess Office of The Methodist Church. Thus began my first trips to Europe, where I discovered a strong presence of serving in nearby schools, hospitals, churches and wherever there was need. The European Deaconess Movement began in Germany with the pietist renewal within the Lutheran Church in the mid 1800s. In Scandinavia and in Germany there are small Methodist Churches, but they also have deaconesses.

In time I became the Associate General Secretary of the Board, and later was elected president of the World Diakonia. This gave me the wonderful privilege of visiting and learning about deaconesses in the Philippines, Australia, New Zealand, and sharing with them in our every four-year World Diakonia Conferences, and other meetings in between Conferences.

(As told to Pat Riddell)

Betsy Ewing
Deaconess 1954-1985
(General Board of Global Ministries Executive)
(The Methodist Church, United Methodist Church)
(Submitted 2012)

Remembering "Love Letters from God"

When I was a small child, my family would spend a few days now and then in a remote hunting Lodge on Racquet Lake in the Adirondack Mountains of New York State. These excursions provided the most fun and wonderful times of my childhood. My first time at the Lodge, when I was about three or four-years-old, was especially significant. We had just arrived by canoe. As we rounded the corner of the Lodge and headed for the back door, we saw standing about forty feet away the biggest and most beautiful animal I'd ever seen--a deer. Daddy took my hand and together we stood there for the longest time, quiet and still. I was spell bound and mesmerized by this magnificent creature. The next morning I awoke very early with anticipation. Upon opening my eyes, there was a deer looking in my open bedroom window. I tried to be still and not move, but I did move. Startled, the deer bolted off. I raced to the window in hopes of seeing it again, but no such luck. I climbed back into bed and lay there just thinking about the deer and soaking in the marvel and mystery of seeing one again.

In the evenings, I would sit on my father's lap, rocking in front of the fireplace and staring up at the buck mounted on the wall. Daddy tried to answer my many questions about deer, including, "How could anyone shoot and kill such a beautiful animal?" I just could not wrap my mind around it then, or even now. We spent hours quietly rocking, and I fixated on the buck, especially his eyes. After begging, my dad would lift me up to pet the incredibly soft fur of this precious creature. Though I understood it was dead, for me the deer was very much alive. These three experiences at the Lodge marked the beginning of my love for and spiritual connection with deer.

Through the years, any spotting of a deer was thrilling, precious, and a gift. I'm not sure when the awareness manifest, but my sense was that any deer sighting was a "love letter from God," and I grew to recognize the deer as my spiritual animal or guide. When riding or driving in the country or mountains, I am always on the lookout for deer. Through the years, the spottings have been too numerous to count.

Fast forward, to my last years, 1995 to 2009, living in Ames, Iowa, and prior to moving to BHH. I would get up very early every morning and drink in the quiet world while biking five miles through the Iowa State University Campus and woods bordering a park. In the woods, I would be looking for deer, and often I would see one, or possibly two. Always there was a sense of thrill and wonder as they offered yet another of God's love letters and a wonderful start to the day.

One Saturday night, I'd not slept well, having been awake wrestling with some tough decisions. I eventually dozed off and just about dawn, awoke with a start, sitting straight up in bed. Looking out the window directly in front of me, maybe 25 feet away, stood two adult female deer in the yard, right there in town. I couldn't believe my eyes, was I awake or dreaming? I sat frozen in place for the longest time watching. Eventually, the deer turned their heads, looked my direction, and stared back at me. Then, off they bounded. Amidst all that was happening, I knew God's immense love was with me. It was a sacred experience on that Sabbath morning.

Another memorable deer sighting occurred in January 2001. One morning at work, I was broadsided by the most devastating experience of my professional life. Once I had regained some composure, I left the Des Moines office and started driving the forty miles back home to Ames. It was a cold, bright winter's day and there was about 8-12 inches of snow in the fields. Stunned and in shock, I was crying as I drove through the country side. Then suddenly, seven deer (a holy number) appeared, standing in the snow white field. It was an amazing Holy Moment. Never, ever had I needed to know and claim God's love more than at that time. As upset as I was that day, and painful, difficult, and challenging the next three months were, it was this encounter with the deer that kept me going, living, and working through things one day at a time. Without a doubt this was a most significant "love letter from God."

God has come to guide and bless me many times and in different ways through the years. Each experience leaves me in awe and deeply grateful. Having a spiritual animal is just one of the manifestations. At any time, by simply remembering these deer experiences, I am immediately transported into an awareness of God's constant presence and abundant love. What a gift !!!

Beverly (Bev) Reddick
Deaconess, Church & Community Worker
1968 – 2007
(United Methodist Church)
(Submitted 2012)

The Day They Tried to Kidnap Bishop Lundy

The Communists were leaving warning signs on the trees in the jungle, warning me, "Go home, redhead!" It was a time of tension and strife with Indonesia and the Communists.

When Bishop Lundy came to Sarawak, he wanted to visit some of the remote locations. This day we decided to visit the school in Tulai, six-to-eight miles down river.

Upon disembarking at the dock, two motorcycles were waiting to take us to the school about three miles away. Bishop Lundy's driver was someone I did not know. I had a strange feeling when we began our trip. I wasn't sure why, but I felt uneasy. The Bishop's driver took off with a loud roar, like the start of a race.

My driver was traveling 25-30 miles an hour, and we were not keeping up with him. I asked my driver to speed up, to get right behind the other cycle. This was a slippery, 10-inch wide, raised path through a swamp, about 5-6 inches above the water. As we closed in on the bishop, his driver speeded up again. I told my driver to get closer if possible. He hit the throttle and we took off. I had never driven that fast before.

We were in sight of the school, traveling at 45 mph, which was not very safe. It felt like the Bishop's driver was trying to lose us. When I saw the school, I felt there was no way the other cycle was going to stop. In desperation I shouted, "Bob, get off!" He reacted instantly. Fortunately, his legs were long enough that when they reached the ground the cycle rolled out from under him. The cycle moved on with increased speed. My driver stopped and I got off, then checked to be sure the Bishop was okay. We caught our breaths. I told him, "Welcome to Tulai! I'm afraid you were being high jacked!"

We finally calmed down after our sudden arrival and went to our meeting with the school board. In the presence of the Bishop, they were more welcoming than usual.

When we returned to Sibu, we sat down together, and I debriefed him on our experiences. We had built new channels of communication with the people. We both chuckled as we reflected on what had occurred in Tulai.

James (Jim) Hipkins
Missionary Sarawak, Borneo (Malaysia)-1964-1970
Singapore-- 1970-1972
(The Methodist Church, United Methodist Church)
(Submitted 2012)

Part I

--When I Had Dinner with the PLO

It was in the spring of 1971, and I was in Algeria as Area Executive Secretary for North and West Africa for the Board of Missions of the United Methodist Church. It was my privilege to meet, at their invitation, with Mr. Abu Messoud, the assistant to Abu Khalil, who was an assistant to Yassar Arafat, head of the Palestine Liberation Organization. They were hoping that I could help them have a chance to speak to the American people at the  meeting of the Board of Missions, and that the Board would assist them in launching a massive information program to help the people of the United States know some of the facts about the Middle East[1] conflict which were seldom given in the news. With Liv Larsen, a Norwegian missionary of our Board, as the interpreter, I was eating dinner in the city of Algiers. Conversation was somewhat hampered with having to speak through an interpreter of Arabic and French into English, but one could not help but feel the longing within the people for freedom and justice in their desire to have their voices heard in the world.

The young man who spoke talked about his memories as a child of seven in 1948, how there was fighting in their city in Palestine as they hid under the bed while guns were fired. He spoke of his father being put in prison, for since he was young and of an age to fight, "he must be in the army." (He smiled ruefully, "And he didn't even know how to fire a gun.") He remembered when the Israeli soldiers came into their home and ordered them into a truck. They were eventually taken to the Gaza strip where they resettled, but again in 1966 were driven from that home. He had not returned to Palestine since that time.

The men continued to recount the various injustices which they felt so keenly–the fact that after a limited education Arab students who were frustrated with life in Israel were allowed to leave the country, but their identification papers were confiscated, and they were given only an Israeli pass with no return permit, thereby preventing their future access into any Arab country. Elementary teachers, accused of being *feedayeen* (commandos or guerilla fighters), were constantly harassed, often imprisoned or expelled. The Arabs felt that these

---

1 I knew there was little chance to get into the crowded agenda of the World Division at that date, but the Women's Division offered time on the Sunday afternoon at the close of their Board meeting and before that of the World Division began.

were evidenced by the many bars and casinos being built in and around the city of Jerusalem. "They know we Palestinians are a deeply religious people," said one. "We are not used to having our youth go to such places. But the Israelis want them to go there and accept that type of life, and with no work, no school, and cheap prices, they are attracted." To the meeting of 80 persons to whom they spoke in Minneapolis in October of 1971, the Palestinians told about what they called "a revolutionary new idea," their dream of "a progressive, democratic and non-sectarian Palestine in which Christian, Muslim and Jew would work, live peacefully, and enjoy equal rights."[2]

The Palestinians acknowledged that this idea had been called "Utopian" and that "few uncommitted people can believe it, let alone support and work for it, "for thus they were supporting the concept that of a new country that combined the ex-aggressor and persecuted into one, but they believed it was essential if lasting peace and justice were to be achieved in Palestine. These Palestinians were careful to distinguish between Jews and Zionists. They were not anti-Jews, but were anti-Zionists, because it was they who had insisted upon setting up a separate Jewish state with no regard for the persons who were displaced, whose property was confiscated, and whose lives were lost in order to make a place for massive immigration.

My experience with the earnest Palestinians in Algiers in 1971, and later a visit to Palestine and Israel in 1989, have inspired my commitment, in any way I can, to join the struggle for peace and justice for the Palestinians–which will also bring peace to Israel.

---

[2] Quoted from an address by the Al-Fateh Delegation to the Second International Conference in Support of the Arab Peoples, Cairo, January 28, 1969, in *Toward a Democratic State in Palestine,* General Union of Palestine Students, Kuwaiti Graduate Society, p. 1.

Part II

–When I Visited Palestine

I was sitting in the Basilica of *Dominus Flev* ("The Lord Wept") on the Mount of Olives. This is the traditional site of Jesus' weeping over Jerusalem. As I looked over the Old City, with the golden Dome of the Rock shining in the sun on the Temple Mount, I thought, "How Jesus must weep over Jerusalem today!"

I had arrived in Israel only three days after tragic events on the Temple Mount. On October 8, 1990, at least 20 Palestinians had been killed and hundreds wounded when the Israeli border guards fired at unarmed civilians gathered in the Temple Mount complex after worship at the mosque. I attended a news briefing by *B'Tselem*, an Israeli human rights organization, and the ecumenical Christian service held in memory of those who had died in the Temple Mount tragedy.

Two of our United Methodist missionaries became personally involved in the sorrow and pain of Temple Mount. Romeo del Rosario (commonly known as Romy), United Methodist liaison in Jerusalem, visited the wounded in the hospital along with other pastors. Mission Intern Joanne Reich was acting director of the Princess Basma Disabled Children's Center, opposite one of the two Arabic hospitals. As frantic relatives and friends of the wounded and dead crowded the street near the hospital, Joanne brought buckets of water for people to drink.

Suddenly the boys on either side of her were shot with rubber bullets. (Rubber bullets are large steel balls covered with a thin coat of rubber. Although not usually fatal, a closeup shot causes very painful bruising and sometimes broken bones.) Tear gas was also sprayed upon the people in the street and even into the maternity ward.

During the twenty days I was in Israel I saw a number of sites that are holy to Christians. Thanks to Romy del Rosario I also met some Palestinians and saw the unjust treatment with which they deal constantly. For example, after a visit to the Palestine Human Rights Information Center, several of us were given a guided tour of the Jewish settlements around Jerusalem, built on what was Arabic land. At that time the ring of settlements nearly surrounded Jerusalem, and today they have occupied much of the Old City of Jerusalem and the West Bank, though such construction in occupied territories is a violation of the Geneva Convention. Since 1948 thousands of Palestinian homes have been destroyed and many thousands killed, many of them women and children.

164

We also visited a Palestinian man and his son who had refused to leave their land, and were living in a tent and an old bus. We saw pictures of their house as it had been. After that, the son served us cold drinks and cake that he had made for us. When we left, we were filled with pain over the injustice done not only to this family but to thousands of other dispossessed Palestinians.

Another concern was (and still is) the crisis in the water supply. Israel took at that time about one-third of its water from underground reserves in the occupied West Bank, and restricted Palestinian access to water. Since that time as settlements have increased, with many swimming pools and green lawns, the water allowed to Palestinians is even more limited. And Israel at will stops the supply of water, especially to Gaza.

Palestinians were not accepting the situation passively. In December 1987 an Israeli truck smashed into cars carrying Arab workers home from Israel. Four Palestinians were killed and seven seriously injured. The incident set off an explosion of demonstrations, and became the uprising, or *intefada,* which had the aim of establishing a Palestinian state. Many Palestinians participated in acts of mass disobedience including strikes, tax revolts, and the boycott of goods. The emphasis was on Palestinian self-sufficiency at all levels.

In a visit to the YWCA in East Jerusalem we saw a nursery school for four-six-year-olds, and business and homemaking courses for women. From there we went to visit the Anglican St. Luke's Hospital in Nablus. Our guide was the then Bishop Samir Kafity of the Anglican Diocese of Jerusalem and the Near East. While there we visited with Salwa, a second-generation refugee in a refugee camp. She had three children who were growing up as refugees. She was trained in social work, but had only recently found work, after seven years without. She told of the frequent curfews enforced by the Israelis, sometimes lasting as long as 30 days. During curfew a person cannot leave the house. Even opening a window or door invites gunfire from the soldiers. Palestinians under curfew cannot go out to buy food. Fresh foods cannot be kept for two weeks or a month. Even if it could, most people cannot afford to buy food in large quantities. Salwa also told of how soldiers often enter Palestinian homes at any time, day or night. Sometimes they destroy the houses and their contents. The soldiers attack, and often arrest, Palestinian men and boys. Is it any wonder, I thought, that the boys and young men are throwing stones at the soldiers? It is the only way they have to retaliate–even though they often go to prison for it. In prison they can be subjected to solitary confinement, even torture.

We went with Bill Warnock, area director of World Vision, to another private hospital. He was looking for a friend who, he had heard, had been injured by Israeli soldiers. The man was in a ward where young men wounded in the *intifada* were treated. There, we learned his story.

Warnock's friend was a nurse. He had been going to work during the recent curfew. (Medical personnel carried passes allowing them passage.) He was hurrying so as not to be late when some Israeli soldiers told him to stop. He didn't hear them, so they shouted, "Stop, or we'll shoot!"

The nurse showed the soldiers his identification card (which all Palestinians in the occupied territories must have). He also showed his special pass. "The soldiers threw them on the ground," he said, "and began to beat me around the head and arms. Finally, they shot me three times in my leg at close range with rubber bullets. It will be months before I will be able to work." He was in obvious pain. Even so, with true Arab hospitality, he offered us candy bars that someone had given him.

One of the 11 patients in the ward was only 13 years old. Another was 17. All had been beaten and shot in arms, legs, or stomachs. There were several fractures. One young man will never be able to bend his elbow or use his right arm again because a nerve was damaged by the beating he received. All the patients were young except for one man who had been shot in the head while picking his olives. Israeli soldiers were trying to prevent farmers from harvesting olives, their main and often only source of income. I wept when I thought of how some of my tax money was supporting these abuses.

All Israelis do not support their government's policies. I met with Roni Ben Efrat, a journalist and activist in the Israeli peace movement. Her newspaper had reported what was happening in the occupied territories. As a result, she and other editors had been imprisoned–one for as long as 30 months. Many times they were in isolation and were *psychologically* tortured and mistreated. (Arabs, but not Jews, are also *physically* tortured.). Once an Arab friend was tortured when the Israeli prisoners could hear his screams. Then they were told that they were the cause of their Arab friend's torment–because they would not confess.

Roni was one of the "Women in Black," a spontaneous, grass-roots movement of Israeli women who every Friday from 1:00 p.m. to 2:00 p.m., gather at Frances Square in Jerusalem. They are dressed in black and they hold signs that say "No to Occupation." Silently they stand, old and young, as a protest against occupation. Every day other people, often dressed in white, come to oppose them. Often the opponents hurl sexist epithets. Sometimes they spit or throw eggs at the protestors. But the vigil continues each Friday. At the time I was there the vigil had spread to 32 different places throughout

166

Israel. There were also groups standing silently in front of Israeli embassies in other countries and cities. [This movement is now observed in many places in the United States, including in Asheville.] The prayers for peace with justice continue around the world.

In the 23 years since my visit Israel has occupied a large portion of Palestine, dividing the country so that life is extremely difficult. Gaza is even worse–a prison from which people can seldom leave, and in which all aspects of life are controlled. Unfortunately, in the U.S. little of the truth about Palestine appears in the media. The possibility of a Palestinian state seems impossible. In spite of our country's supposed stand for human rights, what is happening in Palestine is ignored and our government sends billions of dollars each year to Israel, and supplies planes and arms which are terrorizing the Palestinian inhabitants of the unlawful occupied territory.

[Romeo del Rosario was previously a missionary in Sierra Leone, has also served the United Methodist Church as a missionary not only in Palestine, but in the Philippines, and is now in Cambodia. Deaconess Joanne Reich until recently was serving on the staff of the Scarritt-Bennett Center in Nashville.]

Esther Megill
Missionary Sierra Leone 1950-1962

McCurdy School, Santa Cruz, New Mexico
1966-1968
Area Executive Secretary North and West Africa
1968-1972
Ghana—1973-1980
Mission Interpreter Southeastern Jurisdiction—
1980-82
Mississippi-1982-89

(Transferred to Deaconess relationship 1983)
Volunteer in 5 countries in Africa—1989-1990
(Evangelical United Brethren Church, United Methodist Church)

(Submitted 2013)

My Adventure with Pink Camellias

Deaconess Esther Jones likes to talk about when she was teaching Physical Education at Vashti School in Thomasville, Georgia. She says, "We had no set facility for Phys. Ed. when the girls decided that they wanted to try basketball. We had green gym suits. They were either too big or too small, but I wore mine with pride.

"This must have been in January, and the camellias were blooming. Lots of blooms had fallen off the trees on to the wet grass.

"I realized that there were enough pink camellias to line off the court so we could play basketball on the grass. We did not play much basketball, but we surely enjoyed those lines of pink camellias.

"We were very careful to leave enough blooming pink camellias for Miss Edgerton and Miss Coger to enter them in the flower show. They continued to enter flowers in the shows even after they came to Brooks-Howell Home."   (As told to Ann Janzen)

Esther Jones

US 2—1954-1956 Vashti School, Georgia

(Continued there 1957-1967)

Commissioned a Deaconess 1958

Harwood School, Albuquerque, NM 1967-1971

Brooks-Howell Home Receptionist 1981-1988

(The Methodist Church, United Methodist Church)

(Submitted 2014)

People I Met in Passing

Some of my most memorable and interesting experiences on the mission field involve people met in passing.

The church we served in Santa Cruz, Bolivia, was next door to an overgrown lot owned by the church. It boasted a surrounding wall with a small lean-to in one corner. One day a couple of Chilean men came by asking if they might camp out there while looking for odd jobs to earn enough to continue their journey. The company that employed them in Chile had promised them jobs at the next site--the only problem being that the site was in Brazil, so they were trying to work their way across the continent. They stayed a week, cleaning up our grounds beautifully and leaving delightful memories with our sons and their friends of daily soccer matches.

This was mid 1960s so we were able to pay them enough to take the train into Brazil. We have always hoped that these pleasant, hard-working young men were able to make the schedule for their new construction jobs.

My Uruguayan memory is of two young women who showed up on our doorstep one evening as I was preparing dinner. LeGrand went out to see what they wanted and returned saying that they seemed giddy and might be on drugs. As it turned out, they were simply so exhausted they could hardly place one foot in front of the other. They were students at the University of Venezuela which was closed due to strikes (not an uncommon Latin American occurrence in those days) and were backpacking to Buenos Aires for Christmas. They were afraid to sleep in the open for fear of having their packs stolen and were looking for a safe place to spend the night. Protestant churches were high on the list of safe places! No telling how long it had been since they had slept and I invited them to use our guest room. They refused food, although one did accept a cup of coffee, and went straight to bed at about 6:00 p.m.

When we had heard no sound from either girl by noon the next day, I began to wonder if they were OK. They were and turned out to be charming young women who joined us for lunch. One was Venezuelan; the other the daughter of a Spanish diplomat working in Venezuela. They were to meet the Venezuelan father in Buenos Aires for a flight back home.

Esquel, Argentina is a long way from everywhere and hospitality to strangers is a "given." So when a young couple arrived on our doorstep one day we were not surprised. Neither of them spoke a word of Spanish, but the man was fairly fluent in English. After some halting conversation, we allowed them to occupy a storeroom behind our parsonage, and they were more than pleased with the bare floor accommodations.   They had hiked through the tropics to arrive in the Argentine Patagonia, giving away their blankets and warm clothing which seemed like excess baggage in the heat.   However, that was not an auspicious preparation for hiking through southern Argentina where few days ever rise to our idea of summer temperatures.   They were elated to find a bag of used clothing (for giving away) in their "bedroom" and asked to appropriate sweaters and long-sleeved shirts to replenish their wardrobe.

We saw little of the girl during the two days they stayed, but the English-speaker was so hungry for conversation that he nearly talked us to death.   He was German, and I do not remember if we ever discovered the girl's nationality.   She appeared when they were leaving with her long straight hair on the left and a completely shaved head on the right, souvenir of her stay in an Asian convent.   According to her companion, she always camouflaged the shaved head until they secured lodging, having found that the unusual hairdo prejudiced folks.

I have often wondered if, how, and where these two "wanderers" ever settled into a normal life style and if they remained together.

Jayne Shouse Smith
Missionary Bolivia 1952-1973 Uruguay 1977-1981,
Argentina 1982-1991
New Mexico 1974-1977
After 1991 Special Assignments New York,
Bolivia, Argentina

(The Methodist Church, United Methodist Church)

(Submitted 2014)

My Possessions

(Mission work produces surprises of profound significance. This story recounts how while undertaking a move from one assignment to another I experienced a paradigm shift resulting in deeper understandings about material and spiritual possession.)

Working well past midnight I ran out of energy and time. My careful packing was too slow against the deadline. Too much remained undone, but I had to vacate my apartment the next morning, another hot summer day. I had a "Plan B" scenario ready, to call for help to finish clearing everything out. As they promised, the small standby crew of friends came promptly midmorning. Each one got to work cleaning a room, emptying the basement, finishing the packing, labeling boxes, or moving all boxes to one of three designated places: to the trash dumpster, to a pick-up truck to store in a friend's basement, or to my car to go with me.

It was an exciting time accompanied by some anxiety about the adventure just beginning. I'd drive from St. Joseph, in northwest rural Missouri, to Memphis, Tennessee by day's end.

My mother had driven from mid-state to be of help at the apartment. Grateful for her support and packing skills, I settled Mom in a comfortable place, and put her to work packing a box of my chosen items, one fit for my two-armed carrying capacity. To her I entrusted packing the answer to my question: Other than food, if I had to survive only with the contents of two suitcases and one medium size box, what is most important to have with me? Using this mental image, I judged and reduced possessions essentially to the basics. I had been advised that I would have very limited private space in Memphis.

Before the crew began to work, we met in my bedroom for specific instructions. I stated that only things directed to this room would go into the car. It was emphasized a "treasure box," the one my mother was packing, would go in the northwest corner alone, and no one was to move it. I would put it in the car when all was finished for leaving the apartment.

The treasure box was for things of practical or symbolic importance, irreplaceable items, those of sentimental value, including photographs of family, friends, and objects favored or from my sacred places. In went small souvenirs and gifts as tokens of great memories, the Bible my pastor father signed and presented in my youth. A hymnal inscribed by my mother, an accomplished musician and hymnologist. My hobby camera and other things

171

were included until it was filled, sealed, and I placed it alone in the designated bedroom corner.

Finally, all belongings were packed and it was time to leave, time to get the treasure box. I whipped around the corner and through the door. Stunned at first glance, I sucked a shocked breath. The box was gone! In an instant mental flash I wondered: Who moved it? How could this have happened? Is it in the trash, storage, or my car? Why hadn't I kept closer watch over it? Dumbfounded, my feelings didn't register anger, but angst and heartsick pain did. These friends were not the kind to pull pranks or lie in such a situation. Gathering them, I asked if anyone remembered moving the cardboard treasure box from that designated corner. They all denied moving it, but scattered to help search the vacated rooms.

A look at my watch made clear it was too late to search for the treasure box in the three directions it could be. The crew was finished. I had to start on the road immediately to avoid sleeping in an unfamiliar place in route, and also folks in Memphis were awaiting my evening arrival. I was already an hour behind. So, I had to leave without finding that box. My friends and mother sent me off that afternoon with prayers, blessings and encouragement. I like driving. Yet increasingly, the unfamiliar scenery of southeast Missouri and eastern Arkansas aroused a sense of caution and being alone. Whatever sights I found interesting before nightfall, my mind kept diverting to the lost box. Mentally, I re-inventoried the items it contained. It took lots of advanced thinking to prioritize contents for the box. After all, they reflected the pathway of my life. They were as tools sustaining me, akin to a survival kit.

When arriving at Memphis, I would join a household, city, region, and work, all to be shared with three Christian families, including small children, all unknown to me. As a late thirties single adult I viewed this move with confidence and also as a challenge. The adventure was a personal experiment in communal household daily life and service. All residents were focused on a mission of human development in urban and rural settings of "the South," made possible through voluntary mutual support arrangements, shared tasks, and individual financial equality. In a large house, among multiple second floor rooms for its residents, a small unadorned bedroom, private space, awaited my occupancy.

Very tired, though not yet sleepy, somewhere in rural Arkansas and this dark night I missed an inner sense of location and direction. I moved from inner calm to inner turmoil, the hard emotional swings catching me off guard. I might never have the treasured possessions again; they could be in the dumpster.

Blinded by hot sobbing tears that dripped off my cheeks, I pulled onto a roadside shoulder. I yelled at myself because I had left the box unsupervised while everything was removed from the apartment. Remembering all I was leaving behind, loved ones and years of the ministry work I loved, thoughts of the box dredged up sharp heartaches.

Now, with a fuller realization of multiple losses, I questioned: "Why is this so different and difficult after I've done well with other relocations and challenges?" I grew still as the lyrics of a familiar hymn came to mind: "Fear not, I am with you, O be not dismayed, for I am your God and will still give you aid."

A calm and clarity returned. I felt assured this move was the right thing to do. But how would I deal with life's uncertainties without the tools in my treasure box? My possessions provided a frame of reference to cope with new situations. Facing this separation, I had to relinquish them all and accept total detachment. Finally, I came to terms with this loss. It was made clear: only God sustains me, not material possessions.

Driving on, a distant dim yellowish sky glow shaped the horizon that signaled my approach to the Memphis urban setting. I drove talking aloud, "God, I feel vulnerable with the tangible parts of my identity gone. Help me find anchors of meaning, relationships, and symbols for life there." By the time I crossed the signature bridge spanning the Mississippi River from Arkansas to Tennessee, a spiritual paradigm shift had occurred. I had gained new peace and a crucial life lesson.

I was relieved to reach the destination address. Two of its residents were there to give a warm welcome and offer to help carry my belongings to the second story bedroom. Now about midnight, and burdened by fatigue, I accepted the assistance. I felt hampered without an outside light for unloading the car in pitch-black darkness.

Returning alone to lock the emptied car, my eyes caught the dim outline of something. I stretched hard inside and pulled it to my chest to carry with both arms. This one aroused my curiosity. Then I recognized it, the box of lost treasures! Stunned into long silence, I finally spoke. "Hello. There you are! I'm glad to see you, but I don't need you anymore."

A voice from an unseen source clearly said: "Now that the box no longer possesses you, you may possess the box." I whirled round but saw no one. It was a moment of mystery. Where did the voice and that message come from? Then I smiled, understanding. "It's nice to have you again, old friends. Let's go upstairs. Tomorrow we'll be settled in here."

Mary Z. Longstreth

.S. 2 1962-1964

Wesley Foundation Methodist Campus Ministry

Deaconess 1971-2011 (various appointments)

1988-2005 HIV-AIDS ministries

Diaconal Minister 1977

Church and Community Worker 2005
(prison and community reintegration)
Retired 2011
(The Methodist Church, United Methodist Church)
(Submitted 2014)

30 Days in an Ancient Land

What a privilege to spend thirty awesome days in a land with thousands of years of human history and wisdom. India dismays, amazes, and provides opportunities to connect with the depth of human dignity and integrity supported solely by self-worth, family, community, faith and material support for life to be sustained if not comfortable. Time has an elusive quality in India for buses, trains, and government officials, villagers, and yes, even impatient Western visitors. When you live in the shadow of many centuries of human history, time isn't lived with frenetic life or death urgency but a suspended moment to be savored and revered.

My Indian colleague, Aswar and I traveled by bus to seek introductions to village leaders in the state of Maharastra, north of Mumbai, India, by government officials. We hoped the village leaders might be interested in joining 1,000 other villages in the state to develop a plan for their village using the ideas of all the villagers to create a vision and action steps for the well being of all. The officials met with us and agreed to introduce us to villages who they believed would embrace such an opportunity. We made an appointment with the government official for the next morning and waited. Six hours after our appointment, the Block Development Officer came, and we went to the village. The six-hour delay was explained! The Block Development Officer had a visit from a village leader. Business could not be conducted until the leaders spoke about the health and well being of their families and the families of the village, tea was served and enjoyed, then the business negotiations could begin. No hurry. It was the custom and required time to renew the relationship. Another official from a different village took us for a tour of his district before our introduction to the leaders of the village with whom we would work.

Each village was somewhat interested in the meetings and participated with their ideas, but at the end of the week one village did a work project while the women formed their organization to start a cottage industry. The work project of digging ditches along the streets for water drainage and cleaning out brush blocking the flow of water was the beginning of change and a healing of community differences. Two villages with very different personalities and histories took on their vision and worked together to make changes in their communities. My belief in the power of local people deciding their own destiny was reaffirmed, and I was changed by the experience of authentic cultural differences in relation to time and things.

Marcia Knight
U.S.2 1966-1968

Worked as a social worker in U.M. churches,
in prison ministry and other ministries
Institute of Cultural Affairs/Ecumenical
Institute 1970-1984
(The Methodist Church, United Methodist Church)
(Submitted 2015)

Christmas Dinner with the Fishing Fleet

 When you hear the words "Christmas Dinner," what memory do you have? Mine is of Christmas, 1991, in Dutch Harbor, Alaska. Our small but growing United Methodist Ministry had decided that no member of our fishing fleet would go without a Christmas dinner that year. We had shared a worship service in the midst of a heavy snow storm on Christmas Eve and now looked forward to a sturdy and delicious dinner for all – in The Elbow Room bar.

There was no other place where we could feed our fleet. The only really difficult decision had been where we would provide this sumptuous dinner. All of the suppliers of food had been happy to bake a couple of large pans of rolls, order in some extra salad supplies, or bake a pie or two. One fish processor had even offered to bake four turkeys for us and throw in a couple of hams. When we took a deep breath and approached Flo, the owner of The Elbow Room, to host the event, she laughed, shrugged her shoulders, and said, "Well, they told me you Methodists would change things when you got here. I like this kind of change. I won't serve any alcohol until three o'clock."

When we opened the door at eleven o'clock, we had quite a spread of food on a "church table"; my husband Harry was playing Christmas music on an old piano; Flo was filling glasses with water; the rest of us were decorating the last booth. We looked out and saw men and women approaching through the snow. We stopped serving food at two forty-five and made a tall stack of turkey sandwiches with lettuce and tomato, to feed any hungry people who arrived after we quit serving or to take home with them. Flo rang a closing bell for us, and we hugged her, had a prayer of thanksgiving, and made our way home.

Ann Perry Janzen

Church and Community Worker USA
1968-1983, 1987-1989
Commissioned a Deaconess 1979
Volunteer 1989-1999
(United Methodist Church)
(Submitted 2015)

A Venture of Faith

I remember the beginning of Aldersgate College in the Philippines. It began with $10,000 received from the United States government by the Province of Nueva Vizcaya as war reparations.[1] Mrs. Pilar Galima, the district treasurer and an officer in the Women's Society of Christian Service, felt that the money should be used for a school, since the churches had been repaired. She was one of four women who began going to the church at 5:00 a.m. each morning to pray for a school. The money was used to purchase land for the school, but there was no money to build it.

In 1964 the Northern Annual Conference, at their meeting on the 125th anniversary of John Wesley's Aldersgate experience, approved that a college should be built, to be named "Aldersgate."

I remember Bishop Valencia's saying to me, "Miss Tyson, the women are not going to give up. Will you help them?" Of course the answer was "Yes."

The W.S.C.S. of Virginia Conference sent 3,000 books; Ethel Born's home church sent the first ones. We also received 3,000 more books from Church Women United, and many other gifts followed.

I remember helping to search for a dean. When we could not find anyone, it landed in my lap. Bishop Valencia had asked me to help. I felt like John Wesley as I "went reluctantly to Aldelrsgate."

There were many people who helped to get the school started: hard work by the local people, the teachers and students; Deaconess Manuela Orani, who extended our Home and Family Life Program; and the Christian Children's Fund which helped five hundred children. Miss Orani organized them into twelve children's clubs and twelve parent clubs in different *barrios*.

The Family Life Program brought new challenges as family health was one of the priorities. I believe this was one of the most rewarding opportunities. I remember that I owe the acceptance of the project to Miss Gloria Ramos, one of our teachers, who said to me, "Some of our children are coming to school hungry."

---

[1] *After World War II the U.S. gave money as reparation for any property owned by U.S. organizations which was destroyed*

Aldersgate College today is a graduate college with courses offered by internet to a college in Africa. Deserving much credit are Dr. Johnathan Guiang for his past twenty-five years as president, and Dr. Myrna Vievnes, one of the first graduates, who served for many years as academic dean.

Dana Katherine Tyson
Missionary Philippines 1955-1959, 1961-1963,
1964-1976
1960-Church & Community Worker
Mississippi
(The Methodist Church, United Methodist Church)
(Submitted 2015)

Serving on the Committee for Retired Workers

Serving as staff liaison for the Committee on Homes for Retired Workers for the Woman's Division was a wonderful experience. Getting to know all of the residents of all the homes and knowing that I was undergirded by their prayers was a great source of support for me. There was also a strong Committee on Homes, the members of which were Directors of the Women's Division.

Initially, there were four homes: Bancroft-Taylor Rest Home in Ocean Grove, New Jersey; Thoburn Terrace in Alhambra, California; Robincroft in Pasadena, California, and Brooks-Howell Home in Asheville, North Carolina, though Thoburn Terrace and Robincroft had merged shortly before I began working with the Division.

Reorganization of the Board of Missions in 1964 removed from the Woman's Division the direct supervision of personnel and projects. That limited the Division's responsibility for pensions and health care to those already in service. As demand decreased it was decided to consolidate the homes. Purchase of Bancroft-Taylor by the Methodist Homes of New Jersey enabled those residents who chose to do so to remain there, with the others moving to Brooks-Howell. Following that move the nursing wing at Brooks-Howell was named the Bancroft-Taylor Unit to continue to honor those early founders.

To determine next steps a professional survey was made that included both active and retired personnel. One salient finding was that the retirees were so self-directed and strong in body and spirit that the surveyor added five years to the normal actuarial tables used for his recommendation: "that Robincroft be closed, all future expansion be at the Brooks-Howell site and that the major need of the future would be additional health care facilities."

Mrs. Mary Yaggy, Chair of the Committee on Homes; Rebecca Lyons, Treasurer of the Division and I, as staff, were directed to leave the October 1947 session of the Division where the recommendation was adopted and fly overnight to Los Angeles so we could get to Robincroft before the news got there ahead of us. Following a breakfast meeting with the Director of Robincroft we met with all the residents. After the announcement had been made and many questions answered there was a rather long silence. Suddenly, one of the residents rose and said, "The Woman's Division and the Lord have always looked after us! Let's start packing!"

Betty J. Letzig
Commissioned Deaconess 1950
Church & Community Worker
N. Arkansas Conference 1950-1953

Educational Assistant, Oklahoma, Arkansas, Texas
1953-1961
International Deaconess Exchange Program,
Kingsway Hall, London 1961-62
Staff member of the National Program Division,
General Board of Global Ministries 1962-1995
Consultant, Current & Deferred Giving
General Board of Global Ministries 1995-2005
Involved in many volunteer activities for the Board
and other organizations since retirement
(The Methodist Church, United Methodist Church)
(Submitted 2015)

A Rainstorm with the Scouts in West Virginia

I remember when I was working as a Church and Community Worker a special time I had with a troop of Girl Scouts. The girls usually all went to the summer camp for their special summer event. One year, though, four of the girls were not able to go.

I told these four girls that since they could not go to the summer camp, we would plan an overnight in the Thousand Trees Forest. We would go on a Thursday night, and there would be a good place for us to camp out. It would be fun.

I took them to the Forest. We cooked supper out and got wrapped up in our sleeping bags in the open. We had cooked our supper and planned to cook breakfast, too.

A heavy rain storm came along, and water seeped into their sleeping bags, and they were soggy. I had told them to put their sleeping bags under the pine trees, but they had chosen not to. Now, there was water coming through their sleeping bags, and they were all screaming.

I told them we would go down the hill to the Community Center to get out of the heavy rain. The path was quite clear, and we left our stuff up under the trees and planned to come back and get it in the morning.

We got to the Community House, and the cook made up a big pot of hot chocolate. While she was fixing it, the girls all showered and dried off. Then, they curled up like little kittens on a big couch. The nice thing about the Community Center is that you are still in the woods, and nobody can see you. I got my shower, and we all went to bed.

In the morning, the rain had stopped. The cook gave us breakfast, and we thanked her for rescuing us. We went back up the mountain and got our blankets and other stuff. The girls laughed about how bedraggled we looked. We had had a wonderful time and went home closer friends than when we had started.

(As told to Ann Janzen)

Frieda Morris

Home Missionary 1948; Transferred to deaconess relationship 1953 Retired 1979. After retirement, volunteered in Asian Rural Institute, Japan; Española Valley Group Ministry, New Mexico; West Virginia;

Chattanooga, TN; Choctaw Reservation, Mississippi

(The Methodist Church, United Methodist Church)

(Submitted 2015, age 101)

A Visit with the Aborigines of West Malaysia

In October 1960 I arrived in West Malaysia, then the Federation of Malaya, to spend three years as a short-term Methodist missionary. I was assigned to teach in the Methodist English School in Bentong, Pahang, and to serve as pastor of the English language congregations in Bentong and Mentakab, a city 40 miles to the east.

Just a few months after my arrival I was invited by Rev. Richard Babcock to accompany him, Robert Tobing from Indonesia, and an Aborigine man, Bah-Markus, on a visit to villages of the Sengoi people, one of the aboriginal groups in West Malaysia. The purpose was to see if the Christian faith was alive among the people with whom The Methodist Church had worked before World War II. Another purpose was to encourage the children to attend a Methodist school in the nearest town.

In West Malaysia there are over 150,000 Aboriginal people, the first people to live in the Malaya-Thai Peninsula. There are more than a dozen indigenous groups, one of which is the Sengoi. In the 1930s, because of the concern one missionary, Dr. Paul B. Means, had for the Sengoi people, the first schools for them were started and some clinics were opened in the jungle. Several Batak Methodist workers from Sumatra, Indonesia, were recruited and stationed in centers where the Sengoi could obtain medical care as well as agricultural information and the opportunity to learn to read and write. The Gospel was also shared and many were baptized. The prospect for a lasting ministry looked good.

But the Japanese invasion and occupation of the peninsula in 1942 dashed these hopes. One of the Batak workers and his family were killed and the others were made to return to Sumatra.

All contact with the Sengoi was lost until 1960 when The Methodist Church again sought to make contact. I was privileged to be included on three of these first trips into the jungle to visit the Sengoi.

On our first visit in January 1961 we walked for hours into the jungle before reaching a village where we spent the night after being received warmly and given a meal of rice, fish and large red bananas. The next day we walked further until we reached our destination, a village where one of the Batak missionaries had worked prior to the war. We arrived in late afternoon and spent the night in the house pictured below. After a meal of rice and fish spread out on mats on the bamboo floor, other villagers began to fill the house. By 10 p.m. the house was full. Someone suggested that they sing, so some boys pulled song books out of sacks in the corner. In a few minutes this little hut, deep in the jungle, was filled with some of the most beautiful hymn singing I had ever heard. All of the people knew the hymns from memory, even the children. When I fell asleep around 2 a.m. the people were still singing, praying and praising God. There was no question about it. Even after 20 years, the Christian faith still lived in the hearts and lives of these people.

Batu Tiga Sengo Village

After leaving that village the next day, we walked to another village where we also spent the night. A conversation with the village leaders lasted late into the night with the result that permission was given for Christian workers to come to the village. Not yet able to speak Malay, I talked with several boys who knew some English. One of them, Bah-Rahu,

In Ba-Rahu's House

184

later became the Superintendent of the Sengoi Methodist Mission Conference. I didn't know this until I met Rahu in 1994 when he was with a group of Malaysian pastors who visited the seminary where I was teaching in North Sumatra, Indonesia.

The good news is that the Malaysian Methodist presence among the Sengoi has continued to expand in the 55 years since my rewarding visits in 1961.

Donald W. Turman

M3 – Malaya 1960-1963
Missionary Indonesia 1968-1972, 1992-1995,
1999-2006
Volunteered in Indonisia 2007- 2008
(The Methodist Church, United Methodist Church)
(Submitted 2016)

Is This Your First Time Too?

My first appointment was as Executive Director of Open Door Community Center in Bismarck, North Dakota during the years 1978-1983. The Open Door served a community of families living in huge mobile home parks. There were single-parent families, families where both parents worked, families from nearby Native American Reservations, and a few single individuals in what amounted to a 'city' of nearly 1600 mobile homes.

Through our afterschool program I met the Grayhawk* family. Mr. Grayhawk was a truck driver. Mrs. Grayhawk raised their three children and prepared for #4 which was on the way.

Late one wintry night, someone pounded on the door of the community center, where I and another staff person lived. We were nervous to say the least to have unannounced visitors so late. Finally, I was able to see that there were actually three visitors, all children.

Quickly we opened the door and the oldest boy said "My mama's having the baby and Daddy is out of town. Can you help us?" all in one breath. My associate welcomed the three children out of the cold and tried to settle them down to get details while I went back to my room to throw on warm clothes.

After driving through the snow and sub-zero temperatures, I made it to the Grayhawk home to find Mrs. Grayhawk calmly sitting with her small bag of personal belongings beside her. This was her fourth time after all. I managed to get her in the car and to the hospital without incident, though inside I was shaking with both apprehension and excitement.

The nurses came out to the car taking the mother-to-be to the maternity ward while giving me directions to a waiting area. Hours passed as I alternated between trying to rest and pacing. I do remember how the moon was shining so brightly that February night, reflecting off the snowy landscape.

During one of the pacing spells, the quiet in the room was disturbed by a tired voice. "Is this your first time too?" I looked over to see a disheveled, exhausted young man. It was then that I realized the nurse had directed me to the waiting room for fathers-to-be! I also realized that my pajamas were sticking out beneath both my jacket and jeans. My socks didn't match either.

Mr. Grayhawk made it back into town just in time for his son's birth, allowing me to return to the Open Door to help care for the three older children. I am pleased to report that Mrs. Grayhawk, the baby, and I all survived the experience.

*Grayhawk is an alias to protect the privacy of the family.

Debbie Pittman

Church & Community Worker/Deaconess, USA
1978-1986
Commissioned Deaconess 1979
Bluefield State College, WV—1988-2010
(United Methodist)
(Submitted 2016)

Mission Memories

One of my most poignant memories comes from my very first mission experience, when I was part of a team of three seminary students from the US, working during the summer of 1951 in the Methodist circuit of Herradura, in the Pinar del Rio Province of Cuba. We worked under the direction of Pastor Cesar Benitez, a member of the Cuba Conference. A veteran missionary of the Woman's Division, Miss Dreta Sharpe, was in charge of social work in the parish.

This was my first real exposure to Spanish, although I had notions of the language from study in school. (I regretted not having taken advantage of the opportunity to learn from my Spanish-speaking classmates in the schools of Tampa, Florida!)

Toward the end of the summer, I remained working alone in the Herradura parish. My two fellow students had returned to the US: one of them, Harold, had been to Cuba before and had a good command of Spanish. Pastor Benitez had gone to visit his family in his native Puerto Rico. A laywoman from the parish who was highly educated and had a good command of English as well as Spanish, was also away from the little town for a few days.

In this situation, suddenly there was a death in the parish. The funeral service and the burial had to take place within twenty-four hours. The pastor was absent; so were possible interpreters, Harold and Senorita Del Pino. I was the only visible leader of that Methodist community who was present to respond to the situation.

I absolutely did not know enough Spanish to conduct that service! Nevertheless, I did conduct it and apparently people were blessed.

Years afterward, when again I was going to Cuba to teach in the seminaries, I kept in touch with Marion, the widow of Pastor Benitez, who by that time was living in Miami. One day I called her on the telephone. She said, "Wait a minute, I have someone here who wants to speak to you." Another woman came on the line. "Pastor," she said, "I just wanted to tell you that I have never forgotten the funeral service you conducted for my father that day in Herradura. It was a great comfort to us all."

Sometimes I have said to my very charismatic seminary students in Cuba: "That day in Herradura, God also gave me the gift of tongues!"

G. Fletcher Anderson
LA. 3 – 1953-1956 (plus 2 years - 1959)
Argentina 1966-78 (on national salary)
Peru 1961-1966

Mexico – 1987 (VIM)
1988-1991 (Board missionary)
Cuba –1999-2016
(The Methodist Church, United Methodist Church)
(Submitted 2016)

Times of Transition: Independence and Autonomy

"It was the best of times; it was the worst of times."

Carol and I were blessed to serve in Singapore during times of critical transition, 1963-1970--three major transitions in particular. All could be characterized under the rubric, Independence and Autonomy.

First, there was Singapore's transition from a British colony to an independent city state. We arrived near the end of the "Emergency" in Malaya, when communist guerillas were being gradually driven across the Thai border, and eventually laid down their arms. Communists had infiltrated the Singapore trade unions and Chinese high schools, Chinese-Malay riots broke out, the British military were withdrawing, and the nation of Malaysia was formed, comprising Singapore, Malaya, and the two Borneo colonies of Sarawak and Sabah. This lasted less than two years, as the Singapore Chinese fielded a political party in the Malaysia elections, contrary to the prior agreement which was supposed to allow the Malays to control the national government. Singapore was expelled, became independent, and sought investment from countries both East and West in order to rapidly industrialize and become self-supporting. We were never in danger during these turbulent times, although one of our theological students was critically injured by a bomb blast which exploded on the street just below our college, and I spent most of a night in the hospital with him while he underwent surgery. Thus, during our eight years there, we lived under three governments-- British, Malaysian, and Singaporean.

With political Independence and Autonomy thus in the air, the church was also deeply affected. An agreement was hammered out between the Board of Missions in New York and the Methodist annual conferences in Malaysia and Singapore--Chinese, Tamil (South Indian), and English-speaking--for the formation of the autonomous, affiliated Methodist Church of Malaysia and Singapore. I was editor of the *Daily Christian Advocate* at the 1968 General Conference when autonomy was voted and the first Asian bishop was elected. U.S. subsidies were reduced 10% a year for ten years until the church became fully self-supporting. Over that same period of time, the American missionary force was reduced from over 60 to just one couple. We who came home were replaced by local leaders whom I had helped to train at Trinity Theological College. Eventually, in line with the national separation, the church also split into Singapore and Malaysia Methodisms. And both grew in numbers, strength, and outreach. Today, they send their own missionaries to countries all over Asia.

The mood of Independence and Autonomy also profoundly affected the student body at Trinity Theological College. It began when a Taiwanese theological educator, who headed the Asia branch of the Theological Education Fund, visited out campus, coming straight from meeting with seminary students in Japan at the height of student strikes and unrest. He told of the turmoil there, with students protesting authoritarian administration, rote learning, constriction of student initiative, and curricula and teaching methodology imposed by Western missionaries and educational institutions. In short order our students followed suit. As dean of students, I was called upon to mediate between one professor and his rebellious class, interpret the situation to church leaders, and collaborate with the senior class to develop and co-lead an alternative curriculum replacing their required courses that carried through the final two quarters of study.

It was a heady time, with some faculty upset, others going with the flow, the Board trying to keep the lid on, and irreversible and mostly healthy and long-needed change taking place. Through it all, I believe the Spirit was at work--breaking open old colonial and hierarchical wineskins, letting through the fresh new wine of liberation, and empowering the development of new young leaders for a new nation and a newly-autonomous church for a new era. I am grateful to God for enabling me to participate in this, "the best of times, the worst of times."

Douglas E. Wingeier

**Faculty, Trinity Thelogical College, Singapore,
1963-70
Faculty, Garrett-Evangelical Theological Seminary,
Evanston, IL, 1970-97
Short-term volunteer faculty, theological schools in
Samoa, Korea, Malaysia, Indonesia, Philippines,
Cuba, and Bethlehem Bible College in Palestine**

Breaking Barriers

In the early 1960s I was travelling to Lake Junaluska with three other Woman's Division staff members, one of whom was Theressa Hoover. She and I were to be roommates at the meeting of the Southeastern Jurisdiction Woman's Society of Christian Service.

We flew to Charlotte with a lengthy layover before getting the plane to Asheville. It was noon time and I suggested we find the coffee shop and have lunch. Only as we approached the Shop did it occur to me that Theressa might have difficulties. I quickly pondered "what do I do?" and did nothing. We were seated in a booth in the restaurant and served without difficulty. About half-way through our meal we became aware that their employees, probably 8-10 persons, all white, were lined up behind the counter watching us. Nothing happened, they just watched. We paid the check and went on our way.

At Lambuth Inn, at the Lake, Theressa and I were separated in the registration process as a bus-load of people arrived about the same time. When I finally got to my room Theressa was already there and greeted me with a big grin, "Oh, so they <u>did</u> let you in!" I didn't know what was being implied until she handed me a letter sent earlier to Theressa's "boss," Thelma Stevens. A Jurisdiction officer had written that it would be impossible for a black and a white person to room together, and that Theressa and I were to be told that in advance and make other plans. She was a Department of Christian Social Relations staff member, the Department heading up the Division's work on race relations. Thelma's response was to ignore the letter and let us work it out. We did and as it turned out; there was nothing to work out!

A week later we were all returning to New York, via Charlotte, again with a long layover. Another trip to the diner? Why not? There we were greeted with, "It's nice to see you again; you were here last week."

Barbara E. Campbell
Deaconess, Commissioned January, 1955
Niedringhaus Memorial Methodist Church, DCE, 1955-1958
Woman's Division/Board of Missions (later) Women's
Division/General Board of Global Ministries,
1958-199
(The Methodist Church, United Methodist Church)
(Submitted 2016)